Lib**erty**
and
Justice

PHILOSOPHIC REFLECTIONS

ON A FREE SOCIETY

A Series Edited by Tibor R. Machan

Business Ethics in the Global Market

Education in a Free Society

Morality and Work

Individual Rights Reconsidered:
Are the Truths of the U.S. Declaration
of Independence Lasting?

The Commons:
Its Tragedies and Other Follies

Liberty and Hard Cases

Liberty and Research and Development:
Science Funding in a Free Society

Liberty and Equality

Liberty and Democracy

Liberty and Justice

PHILOSOPHIC REFLECTIONS ON A FREE SOCIETY

Liberty
and
Justice

Edited by

Tibor R. Machan

HOOVER INSTITUTION PRESS
Stanford University Stanford, California

www.hoover.org

Hoover Institution Press Publication No. 543

First printing, 2006
13 12 11 10 09 08 07 06   9 8 7 6 5 4 3 2 1

Manufactured in the United States of America

The paper used in this publication meets the minimum requirements
of the American National Standard for Information Sciences—Perma-
nence of Paper for Printed Library Materials, ANSI Z39.48-1992. ∞

Library of Congress Cataloging-in-Publication Data
Liberty and justice / edited by Tibor R. Machan.
     p.   cm. — (Hoover Institution Press publication ; 543)
Includes bibliographical references and index.
ISBN 0-8179-4702-7 (alk. paper)
  1. Liberty. 2. Liberty—Philosophy. I. Machan, Tibor R.
II. Series.
JC585.L423 2006
320.01′1—dc22   2005029209

Contents

Contributors

ANTHONY DE JASAY is an economist and political philosopher. His published work includes *The State* (Oxford, 1985), *Social Contract, Free Ride* (Oxford, 1989), and *Justice and Its Surroundings* (Indianapolis, 2002).

JONATHAN JACOBS is a professor of philosophy and director of the Division of the Humanities at Colgate University. He is the author of *Choosing Character* (Cornell, 2001) *Aristotle's Virtues* (Peter Lang, 2004), *Dimensions of Moral Theory* (Blackwell, 2002), and other books.

JENNIFER MCKITRICK is an associate professor of philosophy and of women's and gender studies at the University of Nebraska, Lincoln.

TIBOR R. MACHAN is the R. C. Hoiles Professor at Chapman University, Orange, California, and a Hoover Institution research fellow. His books include *Individuals and Their Rights* (Open Court, 1989), *Classical Individualism* (Routledge, 1998), and *Objectivity* (Ashgate, 2004).

Preface

For Plato's Socrates, justice is the all-encompassing virtue of the good human being and a just community is one that shows how the various crucial elements of a society fit properly together. In the modern era, the Platonic conception of justice would most probably be designated to be the virtue of integrity. Justice in the modern era, in turn, is related mainly to politics, to matters of the law, and to the public policies of a country that aim to facilitate justice. Individual citizens can be just, of course, but this tends to mean, mainly, that they abide by the standards of proper community life. This distinction is brought out well in the works of Douglas B. Rasmussen and Douglas J. Den Uyl, where they introduce the idea of meta-normativity.[1] For example, meta-normative justice pertains to politics, whereas the justice an individual may show toward another in an intimate, personal relationship concerns due treatment. Thus, a just or good citizen is one who adheres to the principles of a just society, whereas a friend is being just by acknowledging another's worthy achievements. Like so

1. Douglas B. Rasmussen and Douglas J. Den Uyl, *Liberty and Nature* (Chicago: Open Court Publ. Co., Inc., 1990) and *Norms of Liberty* (College Station, PA: Pennsylvania University Press, 2005).

many other crucial, value-laden, and contested terms, there are many interwoven uses of the concept.

But what are the most sensible, reasonable principles of justice? It is on that issue that political philosophers and theorists have spilt much ink throughout the last several centuries. Hobbes, Spinoza, Locke, Hume, Kant, Hegel, Marx, and Mill as well as the more recent ones, such as Rawls, Habermas, Nozick, and others, have made extensive attempts to defend various conceptions of a just human community. In the classical liberal tradition, this conception has tended primarily to involve some idea of individual rights or principle of individual liberty that a just system of law would identify, protect, and maintain as well as extrapolate to as yet unknown areas of public concern. Classical liberals have focused mainly on the universal condition of negative liberty or the equal right to it, as do contemporary libertarians. In turn, modern liberals, or, as they are known in Europe, social democrats, have focused on the right to positive liberty, welfare, and entitlements, or, to use Amartya Sen's term, capability.

Contributors to the present volume are all convinced, though in their own fashion and sometimes in idiosyncratic terms, that the classical liberal approach is better than other live options. If justice is to be established and maintained in a community, then the first obligation of citizens and the legal authorities is to identify and protect every individual citizen's right to the freedom to govern his or her own life, to live as a sovereign or to uphold individual liberty effectively. Any positive liberty—or capability—that is the modern liberal's concern is, as the classical liberal or libertarian sees it, to be secured by voluntary interaction among citizens: They are to find jobs, health care services, educational opportunities, old age security, disaster insurance, and all other "entitlements" of the modern welfare state without recourse to any coercive force, be this private or public.

This is volume 10, the concluding volume, of the Hoover Institution Press series *Philosophic Reflections on a Free Society.* I wish to thank John Raisian, Director of the Hoover Institution, the Board of Freedom Communications, Inc., and Dick Wallace for their support of this project.

Tibor R. Machan

1

Justice,
Luck,
Liberty

Anthony de Jasay

I. THE JUSTICE OF PROPERTY

How do we tell just acts from unjust acts? The unthinking, reflex answer is often that we need look no further than the law of the land and the judge who is guided by it and, in so doing, sometimes guides it, too. In countries with a long tradition of the rule of law, it has become almost an instinctive belief that the origins of justice are the duly installed legislature and the courts. However, that we readily believe the laws to be just is a contingent circumstance, almost a happy accident of history. In countries with a less fortunate history, people may very well hold that some or most of their laws are unjust and have in effect held them to be so. Moreover, even in rule-of-law countries in modern times, there grew up a widespread conviction that the laws were just in their role of resolving disputes between individuals and between individuals and the authorities, yet unjust in that they permitted and indeed promoted the rise and survival of a social order in which earthly blessings were distributed without regard to desert. Clearly, then, in people's beliefs, law could be unjust; hence, justice is prior to law instead of being derived from it. It is easy to realize that this must be so, but hard to avoid the initial question, to which law could not provide the answer: How do we recognize justice? Where does it come from?

Intuition

It may be held that justice is rooted in our sense of justice. Obviously, if our sense of justice is the result of learning, training, and experience, it would be dependent on justice as it is taught and practiced in our environment, and the proposition that it was the origin of justice would be circular. However, it also may be held that our sense of justice is innate, genetically determined, independent of our social environment. This may possibly be the case, though by exploring the matter further, we might be confronted with the quite plausible hypothesis that our sense of justice is what it is because evolutionary selection, starting in our cave-dwelling days and continuing ever since, has made it so. It would be determined by the social environment, hence dependent on justice as it was practiced. The idea that it was the source of justice would be tainted with the suspicion of circularity.

A deeper objection than this would, in my view, more decisively condemn the derivation of justice from intuitive feelings. Any two individuals may, under the same cultural influences, have the same intuition about a question of justice. In an extreme case, and given great homogeneity and receptiveness to the same outside influences, they may have the same intuition about every question of justice. But just like faith in the rule of law, this need not be so. It is a special case, contingent on circumstances. In the general case, moral intuitions within a given population will vary. This is all the more likely to be so as moral intuitions all too often follow a person's relative position in society. A man entangled in nasty divorce litigation will not have the same views about what is due to women as a man who is happily married. Nor are the destitute likely to have the same convictions as the self-made rich about the morality of property.

Perhaps more awkwardly still, one and the same person is capable, and indeed likely, to have moral intuitions that are inconsistent, mutually contradictory. Writing about justice, I once called these "disorderly minds."[1] In many cases, the inconsistency takes the form of a pronounced egalitarian bias that is not carried to its logical conclusion, but is contradicted by some prior proclamation of principle, for example: "People should be free to spend their own money as they choose. Money should not be allowed to buy a privileged education or hospital treatment." "Families should own their homes, tillers their land, artisans their tools. Such a large fortune is a flagrant injustice." "Labor is not just another merchandise. Bargains ought to be kept." With the possible, though not quite certain, exception of highly trained judges and philosophers, most of us have disorderly minds when forming moral judgments in our everyday life. It would be a hopeless project to deduce a coherent set of rules of justice from such a mass of incoherent intuitions. If attempted, it would be an object of discord.

It has become a habit of the mentally lazy, when confronted with almost any case of non-unanimity, to point to democracy and consensus as the solutions that are second-best only to unanimity and, at least in a world of moderation and

1. Anthony de Jasay, "Justice," in *The New Palgrave Dictionary of Economics and the Law* (London: Macmillan, 1998), 400–409. Reprinted in Anthony de Jasay, *Justice and Its Surroundings* (Indianapolis: Liberty Fund, 2002).

tolerance, that provide sufficient moral comfort. Quite apart from the fact that in worlds of intolerance and ruthlessness they do not, democracy and consensus can at best claim the rank of *modus vivendi*, but hardly that of the fount of justice. If we admit that moral disagreement between two persons is a dilemma, we cannot pretend that the dilemma will go away if we add more persons to one side of the disagreement than to the other, which is what a democratic solution purports to do.

Whichever way we turn intuition and the introspective sense of justice, we are facing intrinsically subjective sensations that are at least potentially at variance. Who is entitled to say that his intuition is just? It is his say-so against the other person's say-so, and the same remains true if instead of two persons, we find the convictions of two halves of an entire society at odds with one another. Nor is their say-so more valid than ours if their half is more numerous than ours.

The principal object of this essay is to propose a concept of justice, or at least a sketch of one, that is derived to a large extent from ascertainable facts about which there is no room for bona fide disagreement and that allows scope to judgments that spring from intersubjectively contestable, intuitive feelings only if evidence will not serve as a guide, in particular, where the "to each, according to . . ." principle rules justice.

To Each, His Own

The Ciceronian maxim *suum cuique tribuere*—"to each, render his own," sometimes also translated as "to each, his due"—is, at first sight, a self-evident condition of justice. It is trivial to say that in justice each should keep or get what is his or what is due to him. However, the condition is quite rightly silent on *what* is his or *what* is due to him. It remains trivially true no matter what specific content is given it. It has been denigrated for being an empty shell that can be filled with any imaginable stuffing. The charge is not altogether well founded, for what the shell does is to constrain its "stuffing" inside a definite mold, rather than letting it sprawl formlessly all over the place. *Suum cuique* is a beginning that gives a theory of justice a definite direction from which it cannot sharply deviate without losing impetus.

A step is taken toward the specific if *suum cuique* is interpreted as "to each, what he *ought* to have or get." The statement that this is what justice entails is still trivially true, but it contains an emphatic invitation to define what *ought* to be the case in terms of some moral judgment or perhaps in terms of a system of such judgments, an entire moral theory. At this point, however, one runs into the fundamental disability that besets moral intuitions and judgments derived from them: Against one judgment, an opposing one can be (and usually is) set; against one moral theory, another can be (and usually is) constructed; and it is then an adolescent dispute to claim that my say-so is better than your say-so. Any decision in favor of one, or even a decision to "split the difference" and bring forth a hybrid, is inevitably arbitrary. Nobody is manifestly entitled to take the decision. Somebody might be empowered to take it, but who is entitled to empower himself or another? And who is entitled to entitle the empowerer? The answer is lost in an infinite regress. In practice, an answer of sorts is fabricated in some political process, where collective choice assumes powers to decide such matters and awards victory to one side or another. The logic and the morality of this process are not exactly translucid. They will be examined in Section IV.

What *ought* to be the case cannot be answered without recourse to arbitrariness somewhere along the chain of reasoning, unless it is deduced from a preexisting concept of justice. Consequently, it is impossible to deduce a nonarbitrary concept of justice from what that concept *ought* to be. It is, it seems to me, the merit of the *suum cuique* formula, empty shell that it may be, to lead in the shortest possible way to this conclusion.

Despite appearances, the purpose of the foregoing was not to show that a nonarbitrary concept of justice is impossible. Instead, it was meant to show how imperative is the need to search for one in the field of objectively ascertainable facts and to exploit the facts that seem relevant to the utmost of their significance. I attempt to do that below.

Conventions

An adequate understanding of both liberty and justice is best reached by first considering the nature of conventions. They are empirical facts, but they also have moral significance due to their voluntary origin and their substance being (tacitly) agreed upon by all concerned.

There are in society—in every society to a greater or lesser extent—conventional regularities of behavior that most members of society adhere to and that virtually all wish all others would adhere to. These conventions arise from the fact that in certain interactive situations there is one behavior that it is best for an individual to adopt if he can assume that enough other individuals he is likely to come across will adopt the behavior that is best for them. If these assumptions are realized, then conventional behavior represents what game theory calls a "coordination equilibrium," wherein no individual can do better by changing his behavior unless the other accepts to do worse. For example, we may have a convention that we do not trespass and do not erect fences. If I then take to trespassing, I would be better off if my neighbor passively let me and accepted to be worse off. He can mitigate his loss by erecting a fence and also punishing me by trespassing over my land. We end up by both erecting fences and not trespassing—another coordination equilibrium, but inferior to the first. In some rare situations, there are several equilibria that are all equally good. In others, some equilibria are optimal, others suboptimal, whereas in many situations there is only one equilibrium, or at least only one that is also stable.

Note that in some interactions there is an optimal equilibrium that is not reached; an inferior one is adopted instead, or none is adopted and behavior is chaotic. The optimum is virtual—it is there potentially, but not in fact. We may be reminded of the social contract in this connection.

One property of coordination equilibria that are actually reached is particularly relevant for their role in serving as the origins of justice: They are ascertainable facts. They mostly stretch far back into history or indeed prehistory, and even in modern times, when the spontaneously adopted guidance they provide for behavior is often superseded by the constraint of statute law, they continue to exist and avowedly condition what people do and do not do. Many do not steal because it is "just not done"—a conventional reason—and not, or not only, because the arm of the law would punish them if they did. The law itself often stakes out its positions upon conventional foundations, which facilitates both its public acceptance and its enforcement. On the other hand, the law, to assert its monopoly, will sometimes seek to suppress a convention that nevertheless stubbornly survives in its shadow. Informal neighborhood associations that "take the law into their own hands" to see to some aspect of local security and order are a case in point.

First Come, First Served

It is interesting to select a single convention, namely "first come, first served," and follow up its far-reaching effect in shaping a concept of justice that minimizes reliance on the subjective, the judgmental, and the contestable.

"First come, first served" is a distributional convention that, by tacit agreement, regulates who gets what when such is not settled by preexisting ownership and auction-type trading. This tacit agreement resolves part of the question of what is a person's own without admitting that after such resolution there may be left to answer further questions as to what *ought* to be a person's own.

If, in addition to its general recognition, further empirical proof of the prevalence of this convention were needed, it may be found in the practice of queueing. Queueing is, so to speak, the small change of the mutual benefit yielded by conventional behavior in the face of a type of distribution problems. The benefit it yields is usually small, which may explain that there is no very evident subsidiary convention among the adherents to provide enforcement and punish queue-jumping. The practice nevertheless survives and tends spontaneously to emerge when needed.

If "first come, first served" is, in effect, a family of conventions, by far the most important of its members for the present purpose is "finders, keepers." The reason is too obvious to need laboring: "finders, keepers" is a solution to the problem of "original possession," sometimes also called "first acquisition," the Achilles' heel of certain received theories of property that accept some version of the Lockean proviso that "enough and as good" must be left for others.

The justice of original possession is strongly challenged by those who, starting from the Lockean fiction that God gave

Earth to mankind to enjoy in common, treat all originally unowned resources as if they were owned in joint tenancy. This fiction, supported by the argument that everybody has the same "right" to these resources as everybody else, leads to the conclusion that resources ought not to be taken out of the universal joint tenancy except with everybody's unanimous agreement. The defense of taking unowned resources into individual ownership, on the ground that the greater productivity of such ownership permits ample compensation of those who are left without "enough and as good" and, in effect, without property, is countered with the very reasonable argument that nobody is obliged to give up his putative stake in the joint tenancy of the world merely because he is offered compensation for doing so. Theories of property that accept a Lockean starting point are, in short, not successful in getting the theory started in the first place, even though if it were to get started, it would serve very well to justify the subsequent growth and distribution of resources by way of voluntary acts.

However, if we eschew a Lockean or any other "ought" as the origin of property and stay firmly on the "is" that alone holds out the prospect of an objective concept of justice, the convention of "finders, keepers" offers itself in the plainest possible manner. Once free agricultural land is all taken up, other resources, no doubt not "as good," may be left. Undiscovered resources are unowned, possibly subject to agreed royalties payable to the owner, if there is one, of the surface under which subsurface resources may lie. By the convention, the finder who discovers the unowned resource becomes its owner (whether or not he "deserves" it by virtue of having incurred finding costs).

Note that there is no rival convention that would stipulate some other distribution, such as "finders share the find with all who have also meant to search but were beaten to it by the finder" or "finders share it with mankind." If such a convention were in fact an equilibrium, it would be a vastly inferior one, if only because few would put themselves to great trouble to search and discoveries to share would be sparse.

The Presumption of Title

The justice of first acquisition of previously unowned resources is established, as a matter of mutually agreed-upon convention, namely, "finders, keepers." It remains to establish the justice of what we might call "secondary" acquisition, that is, the acquisition by its present owner of any resource that he has not discovered himself, but that has already been owned by at least one previous owner. Obviously, the immense majority of property falls into this category.

An abstract general statement may not convey very well the nature of all secondary acquisition, for it is apt to focus the attention on only one type of change of ownership, namely, the trading of objects or claims from hand to hand in bilateral voluntary transactions. Ownership arising from the transformation of labor and material objects into different objects, some of which may be consumed but others of which may be saved and enter the category of property, risks being left out of account.

Some recent attempts to justify secondary acquisition employed two somewhat different arguments to deal with exchange and with production. Exchanges against value received, bequests and gifts giving rise to the transfer to a new owner of a previously owned resource or claim result in said resource or claim becoming the new owner's justified property if the transaction was free of force or fraud. By contrast, the acquisition of a resource through the application of labor (e.g., the sale of labor in exchange for wages or the use of labor in making objects out of bought materials) is justified not by the mutually agreed-upon nature of the activities involved, but by appeal to the curious principle of "self-ownership." Because the provider of labor owns himself, he also owns his labor power and everything he could procure for himself by applying it (again assuming the absence of force and fraud).

The latter seems to be a wholly unnecessary argument and, in view of the bizarre notion of self-ownership that it involves, an undesirable one. Ownership is a relation between an owner and the thing he owns, a liberty of the owner to use and dispose of what he owns. It is outlandish to talk of a relation between a person and his self. It is worse to imply that this person can somehow dispose of his self in exchange for some other self or some other resource. Nor is it much more sensible to suppose that though he cannot dispose of his self, he can divide his self into parts and dispose of some of it (his capacity to work?) and keep the rest. It would be simpler, and quite sufficient, to say that a person capable of producing some labor service is at liberty to sell the service if this liberty is not opposed by a sufficient reason, just as the owner of some other type of resource is at liberty to sell it subject to the same proviso, that is, absence of sufficiently grounded opposition. What a person acquires in exchange for services is no less his than what he, or another, acquires in exchange for anything else of value. The reader will understand that by thus justifying the secondary acquisition of property, one is justifying the freedom of contract. Like any other liberty, contracting is an act that is just because no sufficient, objectively compelling reason speaks against the freedom of parties to agree upon bargains with each other. It must be accepted as just unless and until good, verifiable reason is found to oppose it.

Thus we reach the nub of the matter. The justice of property can be derived from "first come, first served," starting with first and moving to secondary acquisition, entirely from factual evidence—the fact of a certain convention, the fact of possession, the fact of exchange—evidence that is open to objective scrutiny. It is obviously possible to challenge the justice of property derived in this, as in any other, manner and claim that it creates no or defective title. Defenders of property and of what is called the capitalist order have always felt the need to respond to such challenges. Some of these defenses were consequentialist: They argued (quite rightly) that the institution of property and the freedom of contract immensely enhance wealth and welfare and that (less evidently) they are therefore morally justified. This defense is vulnerable to the well-known thesis that it is impossible to judge greater wealth to be better than lesser wealth without also judging that its distribution is not worse. Involving as it does interpersonal value comparisons, such judgments can never be conclusive. The deontological defense of the capitalist order is immune to this riposte, for it does not choose to be judged on its consequences for welfare, liberty, or some other value, but on the legitimacy of property that arises from mutually agreed-upon transactions. Apart from its weakness with respect to the first acquisition of unowned resources, this defense has much to commend it, except that it signifies an admission that a defense is needed in the first place. Such an admission is uncalled-for.

A claim that owners are not entitled to hold the property they do or, less radically, that particular titles to very unequal property are not valid is by its general nature unfalsifiable. This being so, the owner of property can no more refute such a claim than an accused can refute the charge that he is guilty. Falsification is logically impossible, but verification is at least logically possible, though of course it may or may not be successful in practice. It follows that the burden of proof cannot rest with the owner (or the accused), but can rest with the challenger. And until the challenger succeeds in discharging it, property enjoys the presumption of good title just as the defendant enjoys the presumption of innocence. It is perhaps worth remarking that the two are really special applications of a more general presumption, that of liberty.

The presumption springs, not from any moral consideration, but simply from the epistemology of validating a descriptive statement and the asymmetry between two ways of doing it, namely, verification and falsification.

The upshot for my present purpose is that it is not for the owner to prove that he is entitled to the property he holds. It is for challengers to prove that they—or the less-well-off on whose behalf they plead—are entitled to take part or all of it away from him.

II. THE JUSTICE OF EQUALITY

Of the many and, as we have noted, often disorderly and incoherent intuitions about justice, the demand for some kind of equality is probably the most persistent. In the present section, I shall attempt to circumscribe the somewhat precarious and hard-to-define place equality can have in a concept of justice that is, for its property-based part, derived from verifiable facts and that does not recognize the absolute moral superiority of one subjective view of what is just over another.

Distributive Justice

Contrary to the view that there is no such thing as distributive justice unless somebody is actually distributing as well as to the confused and confusing view that there is justice on the one hand and distributive, or "social," justice on the other, all justice is distributive. Most, though not all, benefits are earned and received and burdens assumed and discharged by individuals as the outcome of interactions between them. Present distributive shares are determined by the acts (and omissions) of everyone, past and present. The accumulation and present distribution of capital, the deployment of productive labor, and the income streams generated in the course of production and exchange are the results of these individual acts. Just acts give rise to just distributions, unjust acts to unjust ones. Although "nobody distributes," a just distribution can be ascribed to the rules of justice, and deviations from it to specific violations of these rules. In principle, injustices of distribution are traceable to particular unjust acts, even if the practical difficulty of doing this for acts dating back to a distant past, as well as considering the time discount that should apply to them, justify some measure of prescription.

The acute reader will long have noted, however, that all of the above stems from the basic rule of justice "to each, his own," under which individuals exercise their liberties and rights in commanding their own property and entering into contracts of exchange. "To each, his own" determines the distribution of everything that belongs to somebody. However, there are benefits and burdens that do not belong to anybody in such a matter-of-ascertainable-fact way. At best, they "ought" to belong to someone as a matter of judgment in the same way as other, intuitively felt "oughts" may function. However, they will not belong de facto to anyone until and unless they are actually allocated to him. The student must receive his grade, the artist his prize, the hero his medal, the criminal his sentence. These rewards or punishments are not churned out automatically, without deliberate action on anyone's part, the way income and wealth are churned out as the effects of employing property and contract. They are deliberately distributed, and their distribution may or may not be just.

To Each, According To . . .

In Section 1, dealing with the arbitrariness of moral intuitions
and their unsuitability to serve as sources of justice, I argued
that a concept of justice worthy of the name must not be dependent on moral claims because any such claim can be contradicted by rival moral claims and is condemned to be incon-
clusive.

However, once we have to deal with matters that "do not
belong" to some person in the way property does, and therefore cannot be brought under the competence of the maxim
of "to each, his own," the purist requirement of deriving justice
from the facts of cases rather than from judgments about cases
can no longer be wholly respected. An element of subjective
judgment must be allowed to enter, but its role will be con-
strained by some objective conditions. An example may make
this clear.

A gang of day laborers will exert themselves over and
above their normal pace of work to bring in the harvest before
bad weather hits it. The landlord wishes to reward their loyalty
by giving them a gratuity and tries to satisfy distributive justice
in fixing the amount each should get. He may award three
piastres to each laborer for every hour he works after sunset,
when work would ordinarily stop. Those working the longest
hours would get the largest amounts. Alternatively, he might
pay two piastres to each laborer for every bushel of produce
he brings in after his normal hours. In the first case, each
would be rewarded according to hours worked, in the second
case according to the result of his work. The general rule of
the landlord would be "to each, according to the relevant variable x." It is left to the landlord's discretion what the relevant
variable is. The question being one of moral intuitions, debate
about it could hardly be conclusive and the choice would have

to be one of judgment. However, discretionary judgment would stop where justice began: The landlord would be violating it if he rewarded one of his workers according to x and the other according to y, or one proportionately to x and the other more than or less than proportionately. For each recipient, the reward must be the same function of the relevant variable x.

This sameness is known as Aristotelian equality.[2,3] In geometric terms, every reward dependent on x corresponds to a point lying on or close to a smooth curve. Kinks in the curve, or points lying far off it, would be marks of injustice. We may note that while Aristotelian equality is understood as proportional, that is, the function relating the reward or burden to the relevant variable upon which it depends is supposed to be linear, there seems to be no strong reason for this to be so. A nonlinear relation, wherein reward increases more (or less) than proportionately as the relevant variable—for example, work or result—increases, does not violate the requirement of justice as long as each worker receives the same functionally determined treatment. This condition would still satisfy what we might call a generalized Aristotelian equality.

A more awkward case shows up in a different example. Four criminals have been convicted, each of a different crime. They must now be sentenced. The first is guilty of petty theft, the second of armed robbery, the third of manslaughter, and the fourth of premeditated murder. The relevant variable is presumably "crime" and a just sentence would have to depend (mostly, if not wholly) on "how much" crime each criminal has committed. There is a somewhat fluid hierarchy of crimes recognized in each society, in which robbery ranks higher than theft and murder higher than manslaughter, though any such

---

2. Aristotle *Nicomachean Ethics* Book V, chapters 2 through 5.
3. Ibid., *Politics*, Book III, chapters 8 through 13, Book V, chapter 1.

hierarchy is discretionary, open to dispute at least in some cases, and varies from society to society; adultery ranks nowhere in the West, theft and robbery may rank higher than manslaughter in the East. Admitting, however, that a historically and culturally confirmed stable ranking of crimes exists, the administration of justice is still discretionary rather than purely fact finding, if only because the ranking of crimes is at best ordinal and not cardinal. It tells the judge that murder is more of a crime, more heinous than theft, but it does not tell him by how much it is more so. Justice would require that here, too, Aristotelian equality should be satisfied, but the quantities involved being rough-and-ready, justice is also apt to be rough.

Bosses who decide promotions, military officers who assign soldiers to duties, teachers who mark examination papers all distribute benefits or burdens that would not otherwise get distributed. Such benefits and burdens do not preexist and do not already "belong" to some owner, but are freshly brought about. Evidently, they are not subject to the essentially fact-finding, nonjudgmental justice of property. They are subject to the justice of equality, which, despite its name, is heavily dependent on subjective judgments about facts. It is in this domain that whim and prejudice can most easily penetrate justice and in which demands for impartiality are the loudest. This is precisely what one should expect when discretion, intuition, and hence arbitrariness play a part in determining what is just.

Equal Treatment and Act-Irrelevance

The lack of solidity of the "justice of equality" must disappoint those who believe that the apparent simplicity of its fundamental principle, namely, equal treatment, should on the contrary make for this part of "distributive" justice to be particularly firm. However, the simplicity of the equal treatment principle is illusory.

The principle tells us to treat like cases alike. Reverting to our example of workers exerting themselves to get the harvest in before the weather breaks, we would expect that treating them alike would mean rewarding "each according to" the same variable, say, the number of bushels of produce each brings in. Seen graphically, the treatment of each would show up as a point on a two-dimensional plane, and the points would all lie on a smooth curve. Looking more closely at the group of workers, we would obviously find that their cases are not alike—no two cases are ever strictly alike—for some find it harder and have greater merit in bringing in a bushel than others. If equal treatment meant taking both bushels and merits into account, the treatment of each, depicted on a two-dimensional plane taking only bushels into account, would not lie along a smooth curve, but would look like a wild, formless scatter. A three-dimensional depiction, on the other hand, would show the treatment of each as a point lying on a smooth plane with bushels, merits, and rewards serving as its three axes. Distributive justice, with "each according to . . ." as its guide, would be visibly satisfied.

On a superficial view, regarded in terms of a single variable, like bushels, there would be inequality. On a fuller, three-dimensional view, however, we would find that equality prevailed.

What upsets this appeasing solution is that cases demanding equal treatment are unlike not in one or two but in a very large number of respects. The features in which they may differ are virtually numberless, limited only by our patience and thoroughness in detecting ever finer distinctions. The fatal effect of this for the equal treatment principle is that no matter how rich and full the account we take of a situation and how many variables we admit as relevant, there will always be at least one more that we have failed to consider and that could be added.

Should we then find, after examining a group of cases, that their treatment is unequal and violates distributive justice, we could always add one more variable, and one more after that, and so on, until we found that the inequality that shows up when rewards are allotted as a function of only n variables can be reinterpreted as equality by imputing reward-demanding relevance not to just n, but to $n+q$ variables, where q can be as large as it takes to explain the apparent inequality that remained when only n variables were considered. (It is perhaps needless to spell out that the same reasoning yields the same result with respect to the just allocation of burdens.)

A well-nigh awesome conclusion then imposes itself. Aristotelian equality is a tautology that is always satisfied if the account taken of the relevant variables entering into the equal treatment of cases is full enough.

Represented geometrically, Aristotelian equality would be satisfied if all cases requiring equal functional treatment fitted into the same space, and this would always be so if the space were given enough dimensions to accommodate every reward-justifying variable.

Escape from the tautology is offered by some agreement to strictly limit the relevant variables that may be taken into account in judging whether a distribution is just. For the agreement to work well, perhaps only a single variable, such as work or need, should be allowed. It is obvious, though, that the choice of relevant variable would be a very large and tough bone of contention. There is no reason that such agreement could ever be reached or, if reached, would be observed.

Equal treatment as the guiding principle of the justice of equality does not resist well the energetic shaking of its logical structure. Where does this leave equality in the everyday sense in which it is, sometimes a little carelessly, so often invoked? It must retreat to its bleak citadel.

"Treating like cases alike" admits, or at any rate does not contradict, also treating unlike cases alike. If, in a universe of unlike cases, all get the same treatment, then two cases in the universe that happen to be alike will also be getting the same treatment. If Aristotelian equality must be given up, the citadel of absolute equality still looks safe, and many egalitarians are probably not at all displeased to abandon the former and make their uncompromising last stand in the latter.

In a sense, absolute equality is the limiting case of Aristotelian equality and could be reached from generalized Aristotelian equality by small steps. Consider a situation of equal treatment of a group of workers whose reward varied only with the hours they worked. They might get three piastres for the first hour, two for the second, and so on until the extra pay given for the extra work grew quite small or nil. Past an initial variable sum received for the first few hours, each laborer would get the same pay regardless of the amount of work he performed. The last step to absolute equality would be to replace the variable pay given for the first few hours with a constant lump sum that all workers would get, even those who did no work at all. The unemployed, the part-timers, and the overworked would all be paid the same. Instead of depending on one relevant variable, namely, short or long, easy or hard acts of work, the reward would be invariant to it. It might be telling to call this kind of equality "act-irrelevant" to signify that in this radical, last-ditch conception, people's just rewards had nothing to do with what they did, but only with what they were, namely, people.

Are Equality and Liberty Compatible?

The analysis of this section, pursued to the bitter end, reached a conclusion that most people, perhaps even most egalitarians, would indignantly reject as absurd. How could justice require that people should all be paid the same whether they did anything in exchange for it? Clearly, applying such a rule would breed an uncontrollable orgy of free riding and would in short order destroy the society that tried to live by it.

That a certain rule of justice would go against the grain and rapidly undermine the social order does not make its analysis invalid and does not refute the logic by which it was reached. If the logic was about right, the very absurdity of some of its implications puts advocates of the justice of equality under a duty either to explain themselves more satisfactorily or to give up their advocacy.

It has ever been the egalitarian position that equality and liberty were not rival qualities of a just society, but complementary to each other, that equality enhances liberty. This is perhaps its necessary condition. In a similar vein, egalitarians often assert that property and contract not only engender inequalities, but are directly destructive of liberty.

To reassure nonegalitarians, egalitarians must reconcile at least three propositions that appear to be implied in what they believe. One is that equality enhances liberty, another that true equality is act-irrelevant, and the third that act-irrelevance would not transform society into a hopeless shambles and would not necessitate a massive restriction of liberty.

The literature of political thought in the past half-century is full of attempted reconciliations of dilemmas of the above type. Interestingly, most have a bias in favor of liberty, a bias that must owe something to a poor sense of reality if not to downright naiveté. One of the most influential of reconciliations places liberty as the first of the two principles of justice and gives it "lexicographic" priority, postulating that no trade-off of liberty against other values is admissible—no amount of liberty, however small, must be given up for the sake of even a great deal of equality. Most of the mildly socialist literature shows a readiness to compromise a little on equality, refraining from pushing it all the way in order to leave some room for some measure of material incentives in addition to the purported moral incentives of good citizenship in a just society. Throughout, it is implied that such a society would function by purely voluntary cooperation; thus, liberty would in no way be curtailed.

The present paper maintains a diametrically opposed stand, primarily on the grounds that once equality is accepted as a principle of justice, its demands cannot really be restrained short of act-irrelevance. Halfway compromises, like most other attempts at having it both ways, have unhappy and inefficient results. If this is so, it is liberty that must be made to give way before the crescendo of equality. Equality will not be confined to the relatively limited area in which distribution requires that somebody should actively distribute: that teachers reward scholastic achievement, bosses reward efficiency and loyalty, judges punish crimes. Driven by people's desire to be compensated for their bad luck and to share in the good luck of others, equality will spread by expanded redistribution that, in its turn, impinges directly on liberty.

III. BAD LUCK, GOOD LUCK

A plausible view of the linkage between cause and effect leads to a norm of sensible speech by which one cannot sensibly qualify any phenomenon as an injustice without being ready also to qualify as unjust some act that may have brought it about. It is then incoherent to talk about unjust states of affairs, characterized by inequality, poverty, hunger, or oppression, without a willingness to name, even if only vaguely, the unjust acts that caused these allegedly, or perhaps truly, unjust circumstances. It is not too strong to call it cowardly to blame states of affairs for being unjust while blaming no one for being responsible for the injustice, a blame that may be impossible to substantiate.

To escape the somewhat eccentric fiction that injustices could be self-generating, one can say that they are acts of Providence, Fate, God, or, in the language of game theory, are moves made by Nature. Such acts appear to us as being strokes of luck and are widely (though not yet generally) taken as the most copious sources of injustice.

Assurance Against Event Risk

The battle against luck does not necessarily start in the name of justice. Though it is likely soon to assume that special mantle, it can very well begin as a straightforward consequentialist, utilitarian good cause. It is held, not implausibly, that if bad luck hits random individuals in society, average welfare (admitting that the idea has sufficient meaning) will be lower than if the losses were distributed evenly across the entire society, hitting no one very hard and the unlucky no harder than the lucky. In this spirit, it is a good thing to use society as a giant mutual insurance scheme against random event risks of all kinds. Farmers in a region suffering from drought, earthquake victims, and producers losing their market due to a sudden violent shift in fashion or technology are all to be made eligible for compensation whose cost is to be borne by society as a whole. Even if the cost is not laid disproportionately on the well-to-do, total income will be redistributed in a more egalitarian direction than if adverse events impacted incomes where they fell.

It is fully to be expected, and history bears it out, that after a few precedents in which compensation is granted to a victim group at the expense of nonvictims, compensation comes insistently to be demanded as a right by all who consider themselves hurt by bad luck through no fault of their own. Compensation and the attendant redistribution become matters of justice, as it were, almost by the back door. There is no particular threshold below which bad luck is not bad enough, but above which it is sufficiently injurious and undeserved, to warrant reparation.

The victim's right to be assured against bad luck, and society's obligation to provide the assurance, logically expand to areas that pass for being event risks, though there is little that is random and unforeseen about them. One such is simply the economic environment, which keeps changing over time for a variety of familiar reasons without the changes being dramatic, let alone violent. Not all these changes are favorable to all, especially if all do not or cannot change with them. Firms and industries will then be left behind and those dependent on them become relatively, and maybe absolutely, poorer than they used to be. The hard-hearted view of such developments is that those who engage in economic activity of almost any sort must know that they are exposed to unwelcome changes in their prosperity and must live with them and ride them out. In the redistributive crescendo, such a view is hardly heard. Since the losers from the change have lost through no fault of their own, they suffered what is ever more widely regarded as an injustice for which bad luck was responsible. They are deemed to have a just claim for compensation.

The other area in which society is increasingly obliged to help those who undergo adverse changes in their position through no fault of their own is "social" insurance (though, once again, one squirms at the use of this word in this place). The extreme example is "social security," the promise of a pension not, or not fully, funded by the pensioner's lifetime premium payments. Old age is a largely foreseeable event (though a minority of persons does die before its onset), and whatever arguments may speak for making it financially as painless as possible, it is definitely not a state brought about, except in a facetious sense, by bad luck through no fault of one's own. By making it, at least doctrinally, a matter of justice rather than of sympathy or social hygiene, it is nonetheless assimilated to the doings of bad luck.

In gradually transforming the idea of mutual assurance against unforeseen adverse events into just claims for compensation to undo all the works of bad luck, no explicit demand of justice is made to undo the works of good luck as well. Implicitly, the compensation for bad luck is to some extent matched by a levy on good luck, for the compensation has to be paid for by somebody. However, the match is far from complete, for the compensation, unless otherwise specified, falls upon all members of society except the victims, and not only on the lucky ones. Compensation would indeed be redistributive to some extent, but a systematic wiping out of the effect of bad luck on income and wealth would not systematically wipe out all the effects of good luck. It would diminish them, but only incidentally.

For treating good and bad luck symmetrically, as equally weighty unjust intrusions that true, comprehensive justice demands to be put right, a theory of justice has long been on offer under the name of "justice as fairness."[4] The main body

4. John Rawls, *A Theory of Justice* (Cambridge, MA: The Belknap Press, 1972), 122, 251–257.

of the theory, including the "difference principle" at its heart, may be left on one side for the present purpose. Its opening move, however, is relevant to our arguments, representing, as it were, the opposite pole to the view of justice I seek to defend.

Immunity from All Luck, Good and Bad

The postulate that starts off the theory is that in order for people's rational choices in pursuit of their individual interests to turn out to be just choices and create just institutions, the choices have to be made from an "original position" of fairness. The choosers can fictitiously be put into this position by assuming that any knowledge of the luck they were born with, now have, or expect to have is hidden from them by an imaginary "veil of ignorance."

The theory focuses on fortunate or unfortunate personal endowments, genetic or acquired. People must ignore not only their material wealth and position, which are in part the result of lucky or unlucky events that happened in their lives, but also the character, strength or weakness of will, innate abilities, and knowledge they possess. It has been noted that if they really ignored all this, they would all act the same way and for practical purposes could be regarded as copies of one and the same person if not simply one person.

Luck plays its assigned part in the theory if it is defined in such a way that any difference in what people obtain in life (specified as "primary goods," but "income" would presumably do, too) is due to differences in their luck. If they were really (rather than fictitiously) immune from good and bad luck, their incomes would be perfectly equal, and such equality would be perfectly just. (In choosing the institutions that will determine the actual distribution of income under real-life conditions in which luck does play a role, people will supposedly opt for a modified equality in which inequality is permitted, but only if and to the extent that it serves the interest of the least well-off. This refinement need not concern us.)

Why does fairness require immunity from luck? And more pertinent, why does justice require fairness?

The answer offered by the theory is in fact its key. You may be cleverer, better connected or a harder worker than the next person, but these advantages are "undeserved" because they are "morally arbitrary," matters of luck.

We have here two assertions that, like other moral judgments, rest only on intuitions that have no greater validity than plausible alternatives that can be readily found. Deriving advantages from cleverness, friends, or hard work is morally arbitrary, but so is the ruling out, or confiscation, of advantages from cleverness, friends, or hard work. Topping such judgments is a meta-judgment that the present writer would strongly commend, namely, "do not make morally arbitrary judgments."

More fundamentally, it is grossly mistaken to imply that something that is not deserved must be undeserved. Lack of an argument why a person should have or get some good does not imply that he ought not to have or get it. "Deserved" and "undeserved" do not exclude a middle that is neither; something may perfectly well be neither deserved nor undeserved if there is no sufficient reason to show that it is the one or the other. It would be my contention that the vast majority of benefits and burdens, advantages and handicaps affecting people in everyday life, particularly those ascribed to luck, are of this neutral category.

Finally, even if one admitted the somewhat arbitrary but rather popular view that fairness required immunity from luck, one question would still remain unanswered: Why does justice require fairness? Indeed, calling the theory that affirms that it does "justice as fairness" seems to tell us that one is the *alter ego* of the other. This can hardly have been the intention, for taking fairness and justice as synonymous would make much of the theory redundant. Fairness is a difficult and elusive notion. In addition to telling us that if outcomes are to be fair, luck must not influence them, fairness seems to involve an array of conditions and norms to which games, contests, trades, exercises of authority, and interpersonal relations must conform. Some of these norms are neither just nor unjust. A heavyweight boxer defeating a welterweight may be an unfair outcome, yet it is not an unjust act. Stealing a good friend's girl is unfair, but not unjust. Always sending the same soldier on dangerous patrol duty is unfair and unjust. Overruling a freely concluded bargain that looks inequitable may be fair and also unjust. Serving all your clients well, but the old ones better than the new, is both fair and just.

These cases and others one may think of, for what they are worth, suggest no constant link, let alone an identity, between justice and fairness. They give hardly a shadow of support to the idea that if being lucky is unfair, it is also unjust, and the lucky, therefore, must share their good fortune with the unlucky and must be made to do so by force in the name of justice.

IV. LIBERTY AND ITS RULES

Liberty shares with justice the dubious honor that most collective abuse of the individual, from regimentation to harassment to spoliation to mass killing, has been committed in the name of one or the other and sometimes both at the same time, the better to assure us that the abuse is really a worthy deed on behalf of the common good in pursuit of the values all right-thinking people must share. Taking the names of liberty and justice in vain, whether out of political cynicism or muddle-headedness, has always been done with remarkable impunity.

Impunity for falsehood or mere sloppy usage by legislators, rabble-rousers, and opinion makers reflects little credit on the professional thinker whose vocation it is to define important concepts both rigorously and simply so as to reduce the degree of freedom left for loose talk, windy ideological meanderings, and tall claims of fictitious rights. Introducing conceptual rigor is often an ungrateful task, for if it is at all successful, its effect is to let the air out of pretty balloons, turn off the sound, and leave the public feeling let down. It is nonetheless the honest thing to do, and it should be tried again and again.

The present essay has tried to bring a little more clarity and discipline to the philosophical discussion of justice. The main object was to make a contribution to the gradual strengthening of a concept of justice that recognizes injustice only if it results from unjust acts. I hope to have shown how broadening the justice of equality beyond its proper scope, by treating the effects of luck as unjust acts, causes all dams to burst and leaves endless swampland that ceaseless redistribution must keep churning up.

Justice and freedom are interrelated—a harmless generality that tells us little or nothing. More particularly, they share a common interface: The rules of perfect justice are also the rules of an ideal freedom. Outlining the essential logical structure of freedom may lend some support for this proposition.

Feasibility and Freedom

In ordinary discourse, "can" and "may" are easily confused. "Can" indicates feasibility, "may" liberty to do the feasible. (In a wider context, we also say that we "may" but cannot do a certain thing. The present analysis deals only with what is feasible.) There is a large universe of acts a given individual is capable of performing, but only some of these acts is he free to perform. The feasible set is physically determined, its free subset socially determined. Descriptively, the feasible set is divided in two by a system of rules. The rules form a fence, on one side of which every act is "may" and free, on the other it is "must not" and unfree.

These rules are either self-enforcing or enforced in some manner, so acts falling into the unfree subset of the feasible set have some probability of worsening the position of the actor due to retaliation by others or by otherwise attracting punishment.

Classifying acts as free and unfree in terms of their relation to actually enforced rules makes it obvious that the extent or quality of a representative individual's freedom in a given society of given physical and intellectual resources depends essentially on the nature of the rule system in force. One rule system gives rise to more, or more perfect, liberty than another. Anticipating some of the argument that follows in the next subsection, we may regard rules as belonging to one or the other of two kinds, the conventional and the statutory. (Judge-made common law is ultimately statutory if the authority of judges springs from statute in a broad sense.) Conventional rules emerge spontaneously; statutory ones are the products of a collective choice mechanism, such as a state.

At this juncture, a definition of individual freedom may be attempted. We may best consider freedom as a relation between a person and an act, such that performance of the act does not render the person liable to any rule-enforcing sanction under the prevailing rule system and such that the same relation also holds between this act and every other person similarly placed in relevant respects. The rule system is complete if it selects unfree acts in such a way that violation of the freedom of free acts is tantamount to committing an unfree act. Threatening to harm by some unfree act a person pursuing his peaceful purposes must itself count as unfree unless he deviates from his intended course, even if the threatened act is not committed. On the other hand, making the person deviate by threatening him with an act that is itself free (such as persuading my tailor to cut his price by the threat of taking my custom to his competitor) must itself be free. Committing an unfree and harmful act is a tort; threatening to commit it is coercion. Coercion is plausibly defined as an attempt to cause a person to deviate from his intended course by the threat of harming him by an unfree act. Legitimate coercion is coercion exerted to enforce a valid rule, that is, to deter or punish rule-violation. Nothing need stop us, however, from disapproving of all coercion except the one that is needed to enforce the rule we approve.

In common parlance, the rich who choose what they will do without being much hampered by a budget constraint, are free compared with the poor. Likewise, the knowledgeable and experienced are regarded as freer than the ignorant because they have a wider array of options to choose from. Both wealth and knowledge increase the feasible set and, with other things equal, freedom. However, it is preferable to treat wealth and knowledge as parameters that make the feasible set what it is, and consider freedom in relation to that given feasible set. This is not to deny that wealth and knowledge may contribute to freedom. Treating them as data when analyzing freedom is perfectly consistent with admitting that if they were greater than they are, freedom might well also be greater. Plainly, however, it matters to freedom how—by virtue of what political or other developments—knowledge and, particularly, wealth, have increased. In short, the relation between wealth and freedom is conjectural and this speaks in favor of keeping separate things separate, taking the feasible set as given and, within the given set, looking for the changes in freedom that are owing to changes in the rule system alone.

This way of proceeding might help to steer clear of much of the mostly demagogic rhetoric about "how to set the people free." It is customary to declare that by improving public education and by lifting low incomes through redistribution, people become free. It is safer and more sober to claim simply that they become better educated and better off. As in any redistribution, there are gainers and losers, and through the contrasting effects on their feasible sets, some may become more free and others less so. This poses an aggregation problem that has as many solutions as there are opinions about the matter. Let us add, for good measure, that while such opinions are ostensibly about freedom, subconsciously they will also be about "social" welfare or utility.

Some salutary clarification of the concept of freedom may be achieved by briefly considering the use of the appalling clichés "positive" and "negative" freedoms. The first is meant to signify "freedoms to . . ." and the latter, "freedoms from . . . ." Consider in this context "freedom of speech" and "freedom from hunger." Both can be written in the same "positive" form—"freedom to speak" and "freedom to eat (when hungry)." The first can also be written as a "negative" freedom—freedom from censorship, intimidation, gagging, and so on. This, I suggest, is true of every conceptually genuine freedom; all can be equally well expressed in "positive" and in "negative" form. This, I believe, is a good indication that adorning these freedoms with algebraic signs tells us nothing. In the case of "freedom from hunger," however, the reversion from "negative" to "positive," namely to "freedom to eat," does not work well. "Freedom to eat" does not translate back into "freedom from interference with one's eating." The reason is that under the false name of freedom, we are shown here a relation that is not a freedom, but a right. I am free to eat when hungry provided I have food (which is trivial) or, if I do not have food, provided somebody else is under an obligation to supply it for me. This is a relation between an act and two persons, one of whom has the right to require the other to give him food while the other is obliged to give it. Some political theorists no doubt have this rights/obligations relation in mind when they speak of "positive freedom." They mean a freedom to requisition resources from others.

Finally, a word needs to be said about the "right to liberty." If an act is in effect a free one, everybody has the "right" to perform it, but to say that they all do is analytic—it tells us nothing we do not already know from the fact that the act is free. If only some may perform it and others must not, the act is not free, but is a privilege. That some have a "right" to it could be more tellingly expressed by saying that some have this privilege. However, it may also be the case that the act in question is in effect not free. It is effectively an unfreedom and we want to convey that it ought to be a freedom. Effectively, no one has a "right" to it. If we nonetheless affirm that all do, we are arguing for the freeing of this act from the "right" to perform it. However, if one can think of a sufficient reason for crediting all with such a right, it is that the act in question would be at worst harmless, at best useful or pleasant. In other words, we ascribe to everyone a "right" to perform it because of its nature, because of what it is. If so, it would suffice to say directly that the act being what it is, it ought to be free. No good is done by inventing a "right" to it, especially as it is not this "right" that serves as the reason it ought to be free.

This is one of the numerous examples where the rhetoric of "rights" is glibly employed even though it is superfluous. It does actual harm if it obscures common-sense understanding and logic. It also offends against minimum intellectual standards by basing the existence of these "rights" on the gratuitous supposition that people have them.

Liberty Under Conventional and Statutory Rules

A convention, or conventional rule, has two characteristics that are crucial for liberty, or more precisely for the formation of the unfree subset of the feasible set. Because, loosely speaking, liberty is the residual left after the rules have selected and taken out what must not be done, our interest is in how conventions select and how they give effect to prohibitions.

The first crucial characteristic of the division of the feasible universe into unfree and free segments is that the convention has no identifiable source. No mind has conceived it in order to achieve an overall purpose serving an entire community. Nobody has invented it, nobody organizes or exerts pressure for its adoption and no authority is needed to preside over it. It emerges by way of individuals choosing, among available alternatives, the behavior they expect to elicit in response, a behavior from other individuals that would be favorable to themselves. These expectations will be governed by what response to each alternative behavior would probably be chosen by these other individuals. After full adjustment that may take place, perhaps over centuries, while a society is in its early formative stages, nearly everybody will have chosen the behavior that is good for him in case everybody else has also selected the behavior that is good for them in that case. I say "good" rather than "best" for each, for there is no certainty that the mutual adjustment will always produce the best possible coordinated behavior, though there is some presumption that it will do so.

The mutual respect for life and limb generates the rule

against killing and maiming, the respect for another's property, and the keeping of promises (the conventions identified as such by Hume[5]) generates the several prohibitions of trespass, theft, robbery, fraud, and default on contracts. In practically all civilizations, the panoply of conventional rules against torts and breach of reciprocal promises is almost identical. It seems to be a universal property of human society that it tends to favor the emergence of these conventions. The incentive for each individual to adhere to the convention is his immediate interest, governed by the rational expectation of how others will, in response, pursue their own immediate interest. This is in contrast to the contractarian fiction, in which individuals agree to sacrifice their immediate interest in favor of a common good that will serve the ultimate interest of all—a fiction that suffers from the implausibility of each individual crediting the other with a willingness to sacrifice his immediate interest. It is hardly possible, then, to sustain the contention that social contracts among rational individuals could be voluntarily agreed upon.

If there is any rule-bound social behavior that is voluntary, adopted by each without being imposed by some on others, it is the convention.

Next to voluntariness, the second characteristic of conventional rules crucial for liberty is that they do not have to rely on any special agency for their enforcement. Conventions that do not involve conflicting motives among the participants, for example, the rule of driving on the same side of the road, are self-enforcing; it is better to drive on the side where all others drive. Conventions that must cope with conflicting motives, for example, "do not steal," where each participant wants the oth-

---

5. David Hume, *A Treatise of Human Nature* (Oxford: Oxford University Press, 1749/1978), Book III, Part II, Section VIII (esp. p 541).

ers not to steal from him while he would be tempted to steal from them, are also self-enforcing, but in a more complex way. Some or all participants must have a contingent "strategy" by which they would retaliate against the thief, and the threat of such punishment reduces or eliminates the temptation to deviate from the convention. The threat of retaliation should pass for legitimate coercion.

A specialized enforcing agency must be endowed with power to carry out its function. The idea of a minimal state, confined to enforcing the "rules of just conduct," hinges on the specialized agency not using its power to widen its functions, not transforming its clients into subjects, and not gathering more power into its hands. Underlying incentives being what they are, it would be surprising if the agency did not use its power in such ways, and it is surprising that some theorists of "minarchy" (minimal state power)[6] tacitly suppose that it would not.

The fact that enforcement under a conventional rule system is rooted in the conventions is totally decentralized and the fact that the power it needs is spread wide over society, being in the hands of the individual participants, are safeguards of liberty. They are safeguards, in that they contain neither incentives nor power for the expansion of the rule system itself beyond the conventional.

Statutory rules are almost diametrically opposed to conventional ones, both as to source and as to enforcement. Their source is a rule for rule making (formally, a constitution, if there is one, or informally, the will of the holders of state power). Under this rule making or meta-rule, a new rule can be created or an existing one changed by satisfying certain

6. Robert Nozick, *Anarchy, State, and Utopia* (New York: Basic Books, 1974), 26–28, 108–110, 131–133.

necessary conditions laid down in it. For instance, in dictator-
ship the rule-making rule is that the dictator's orders shall be
obeyed until he revokes them. In a democratic system, it is
certain voting requirements that must be fulfilled in order for
one part of the electorate or its representatives to create or
modify rules.

Two violations of freedom are involved. One is the illegit-
imate origin of the rule-making rule itself. If it is derived by
reference to a higher rule, the problem of legitimacy is simply
shifted upward to that higher rule, and from it, to an even
higher one in an infinite regress. If there is no reference to a
higher rule, legitimacy would suppose that the rule was created
unanimously because prior to a rule authorizing it, there is no
reason for holding that overruling dissent (e.g., a minority's
refusal to recognize the rule) could be done legitimately. Unanimity, however, is too exacting to be treated as a realistic alternative except in some special case.

The other violation occurs by incorporating in the rule-
making rule a clause, which I shall call "rule of submission."
This clause provides that any rule created in conformity with
the rule of rule making must be obeyed by all to whom its
provisions apply, irrespective of whether they would consent
or dissent if given the choice.

Regarding the enforcement of statutory rules, no explicit
discussion is needed to evoke the impact on liberty of the existence of a specialized enforcer, such as a state. There are
obvious incentives, and an obvious capacity, for it to expand
its area of competence and to augment its power, and no obvious incentives, backed by capacity, to counteract its expansion.

The Asymmetry Between Individual and Collective Choice

Statutory rule making and enforcement jointly constitute a collective choice mechanism (also called social choice) that is capable of overruling individual choices once they are made and changing the scope left for individual choices yet to be made. It is a vitally important asymmetry between the two that what collective choice can do to individual choices, individual choices cannot do to collective ones.

In fact, the only manner in which in a state the relative scope of individual choices can expand is the same as that in which it can contract, namely, by collective choice. The main measure by which collective choice can make room for individual ones is privatization of public assets and public services. The main measures by which collective choice overrules and restricts individual ones are the replacement of conventional rules by statutory ones, redistribution of income and wealth, for electoral or ideological purposes typically with an egalitarian bias, via transfers, welfare entitlements, compulsory "social" insurance, and the targeted production of public goods, where costs and benefits impact different segments of society differently.

Over the last century and a half, collective choice mechanisms throughout the world have become increasingly dominated by mass voting and especially its extreme form, universal suffrage. Both historical evidence and the conclusions of public choice theory support the conjecture that electoral processes strongly influence collective choice to enlarge, rather than constrict its own scope by recourse to the measures mentioned above. This expansion has not been regular; at times it slowed or was temporarily halted in various countries, but even during waves of privatizations, it was never reversed.

To grasp the magnitude of the effect on freedom, let us

consider the rule system one last time. Statutory rules regarding taxation and public borrowing preempt a portion of resources. Their spending is to be decided by collective choice. Removing resources from the feasible set of a taxpayer reduces the number and size of free acts he could have chosen to perform if the resources in question had not been preempted for collective choice. The tax code has, so to speak, transferred these acts from the free to the unfree category, for the taxpayer must not spend what he owes in tax.

Transfer payments will offset some of this effect if the taxpayer is a net beneficiary from them. Benefits in kind, such as "social" insurance and public goods, however, unambiguously reduce free acts available for individual choice, whatever the good they may be deemed to do to material welfare.

V. CONCLUDING REMARK

The reasoning in this essay has been quite abstract and has perhaps tried the reader's patience. I have taken that risk because I believed, and with hindsight still do, that only in this way could I achieve a coherent analysis of justice, liberty, and their interdependence that was general enough to fit a wide variety of possible cases. Ordered anarchy is a possible, though not an actual, case; various constitutions and forms of state are possible; and some are actual. If I put myself in the reader's place, the conclusion I think I would draw as I put down this text would be that the only type of organized society in which justice and freedom are not endangered, eroded, or perverted is ordered anarchy. I might find this quite unhelpful, considering that ordered anarchy may well be possible but is certainly unlikely to occur and beyond our individual capacity to bring about.

Although this is probably the case, the conclusion that only ordered anarchy is a safe habitat for justice and freedom does not seem to me altogether pointless. It might well sharpen our perceptions and our understanding of what is happening around us and to us. The effect upon our state of mind would not be vast, but even a little good would redeem this essay from being quite quixotic.

2

———

The Exercise of Liberty
and the Moral
Psychology of Justice

Jonathan Jacobs

WHATEVER ONE'S SPECIFIC VIEW concerning the legitimacy of political authority, the grounds for political obedience, individuals' rights, or the fundamental institutional arrangements of a state, they will presuppose some sort of philosophical anthropology. This is quite plain in the theorizing of such thinkers as Aristotle, Augustine, Machiavelli, Hobbes, Locke, Rawls, and many others. Political theorizing reflects a thinker's conception of what he or she takes to be (at least some of) the normatively

I would like to express my gratitude to Tibor Machan for providing me an occasion to write this paper and for his insights into the topic. Douglas Den Uyl and Douglas Rasmussen provided several suggestions and criticisms and are owed thanks for their helpfulness and advice in this, and in many other, cases. Their work on the topic has been a valuable guide in several ways. Noel O'Sullivan is to be thanked for numerous insights, suggestions, and observations that have brought into relief important features of the topical landscape that I otherwise would not have noticed. Also, conversation with Michael Moses on some related topics were very helpful to me in regard to the present one. For whatever is unsatisfactory about this paper, I have only myself to thank.

significant features of human nature. Those features are crucial to understanding (and justifying) the theorist's view of the principles, norms, ideals, and constraints that properly order the political world. In what follows I will elaborate on this claim about philosophical anthropology and use it as a basis for the claims that a high degree of individual liberty is justified and that there is a deep connection between liberty and justice. The main overall claim is that rational self-determination makes politics unavoidable for human beings, and the examination of why shows that extensive liberties are crucial to a just political order.

I

A key element of the most plausible philosophical anthropology is that human beings are capable of rational self-determination.[1] There are many kinds of creatures that feel pain, sense danger, can be calm or anxious, and have other psychological states, but without being aware of considerations as having *valuative significance.* They do not endorse (or repudiate) values. They do not engage in practical reasoning that involves taking considerations as reasons. They may move about voluntarily but they do not conceptualize themselves as agents. Accordingly, they do not have ideals, aspirations, or principled stands on anything. Valuative significance is a distinctive and essential feature of human lives, and it and rational self-determination need to be understood together.

By rational self-determination I mean that human beings

1. Of course, very young children as well as anyone when asleep or hindered by injury or disease are limited in their self-determination. Still, a human being is an individual of a kind that is normally and distinctively capable of self-determination, barring extraordinary conditions that impede its development or exercise.

can act on the basis of considerations they endorse as reasons. They can act on the basis of what they take to be good, or worth doing, or desirable, and they can deploy those considerations in judgment, deliberation, and action. This attribution of valuative significance to human activity does not depend upon there being a teleology of human nature if that means there is a common, intrinsic perfection of human nature, a mode of activity, or a state of attainment that is the uniquely proper end of a human being. It *does* depend upon the teleological nature of a great deal of human activity, but that does not, in its own right, imply that there is a particular best one. In acting for reasons, an activity that is an enactment of what a person endorses, the individual is engaged in activity properly described as teleological. That is wide open to all sorts of considerations being regarded as reasons. Also, there is no presumption that agents are virtuous. The selfish or dishonest scheming their way to what they want are acting in a purposeful way just as much as those who are honest meticulously ensure that everyone's interests are consulted. There is valuative significance (for better or worse) in each case. People may have all manner of wrong or perverse conceptions of what it is good to do and why. That makes their actions bad or reprehensible; it does not drain them of point or significance. In acting purposively, our behavior indicates what we take to have worth and what we believe is worth doing.

We should not confine rational activity and valuative significance to decisions and doings. There are also responses, attitudes, and aspects of sensibility that have such features. This is because of the way in which comprehension and judgment are involved in them. For instance, admiration and gratitude— whether or not they issue an action—are responses that involve valuations susceptible to reasoned support and criticism. We judge someone as deserving or meriting admiration or gratitude, and the same goes for attitudes such as contempt and loathing. These and other responses and attitudes are merited rather than being merely caused. Accordingly, they can be appropriate and well placed or inappropriate and ill placed.[2] There are grounds for them, and we can be mistaken in having these responses and attitudes. A reflexive withdrawal on account of sudden fright or screaming on the fast downhill of a roller coaster involves no judgment, no consideration at all. Those reactions are caused without our considering their fitness or appropriateness. (There are also many intermediate or "mixed" cases.) But a great deal of what we affectively respond to matters in the ways that it does because of what we endorse, have concern for, and judge to be noble or base, worthwhile or pointless, fulfilling or repugnant, and so forth. There is an element of cognitive judgment in each of these. They are not "mere" passions, thoughtless reactions, or groundless preferences.

Value judgments and assessments of worth, appeal, repugnance, baseness, and so forth figure unavoidably in a person's life whether or not the individual is reflective. Those who are shallow or impulsive deploy valuations even if they do not examine them. There are many instances in which agents are responsible for what they do or what they are like, even if they do not *take* or acknowledge responsibility for it. This raises a number of thorny moral questions about blame and punishment, but we need not pursue them in the present discussion. Apart from exceptions such as being coerced or defrauded and weakness of will, what people do reflects what they think worth

2. This distinction between meriting and causing is borrowed from John McDowell, who made it in his "Values and Secondary Qualities," printed in *Essays on Moral Realism*, ed. Geoffrey Sayre-McCord. His point was to distinguish between affective responses that are simply elicited without thought or judgment and sensibility that is responsive in ways that reflect judgment.

doing, even if their consideration of matters is shallow or impetuous.

The significance of these claims about the end-oriented, value-laden character of so much human activity is that they help explicate why politics is unavoidable for human beings. We are not only social beings—beings who live in groups and whose lives involve cooperation, division of labor, transmission of knowledge, custom, and the like. We are also *political* beings because our lives are shaped to a large extent by concerns, commitments, and ends that we conceptualize as such—that we conceptualize *as* valuatively significant. Human beings fashion institutional arrangements, relations of authority, and they specify prohibitions and obligations, practices and rules to govern behavior in settled and norm-governed ways. Being political creatures is symptomatic of our nature as social and rational. And to a large extent, goods and interests that concern us as social beings are, in turn, made possible by settled civil and political order. The latter helps secure conditions for various forms of association, for security, for many of the cultural activities, traditions, and pursuits and ideals integral to human lives. We *need* politics. Political order supplies conditions for valuatively significant human activity.

II

Natural law theorizing is a good example of the recognition that we are not merely social, but also political beings. For all of their (real and important) differences, conceptions of natural law are conceptions of the legitimacy of political authority as based upon a view of considerations that (putatively) have a special claim on individuals as rational agents. There are different conceptions of the prepolitical condition of human beings, of the institutional forms that are legitimate, of the powers and aims of the state, and so forth. But natural law theorizing is an attempt to come to grips with the necessity of politics for human beings. It focuses on a small number of crucial features of human beings, and from that basis, it argues that there are such and such reasons for forming a political order of thus and such form.

Natural law theorizing is a way to address an unavoidable *problem*; namely, given the valuatively significant features of human nature and human activity, what sorts of arrangements of governing authority properly answer to them? Consider some examples.

According to Grotius, man's sociable nature is crucial to understanding natural law:

> This Sociability . . . or this care of maintaining Society in a Manner conformable to the Light of human Understanding, is the Fountain of Right, properly so called; to which belongs the Abstaining from that which is another's, and the Restitution of what we have of another's, or of the Profit we have made by it, the Obligation of fulfilling Promises, the Reparation of a Damage done through our own Default, and the Merit of Punishment among Men.[3]

In Aquinas's view:

> . . . it is evident that all things partake in some way in the eternal law, in so far as, namely, from its being imprinted on them, they derive their respective inclinations to their proper acts and ends. Now among all others, the rational creature is subject to divine providence in a more excellent way, in so far as it itself partakes of a share of providence, by being provident both for itself and for others. Therefore it has a share of the eternal reason, whereby it has a natural incli-

---

3. Quoted in Richard Tuck, *Natural Rights Theories* (Cambridge: Cambridge University Press, 1979), 72.

nation to its proper act and end; and this participation of the eternal law in the rational creature is called the natural law.[4]

According to Hobbes, "A LAW OF NATURE [Hobbes's emphasis], *lex naturalis*, is a precept or general rule, found out by reason, by which a man is forbidden to do that, which is destructive of his life, or taketh away the means of preserving the same; and to omit that, by which he thinketh it may be best preserved."[5] "And that which is not against reason, men call Right, or *jus*, or blameless liberty of using our own natural power and ability. It is therefore a *right of nature* [Hobbes's emphasis]: that every man preserve his own life and limbs, with all the power he hath."[6]

> . . . it is a precept, or general rule of reason, *that every man, ought to endeavour peace, as far as he has hope of obtaining it; and when he cannot obtain it, that he may seek, and use, all helps, and advantages of war.* The first branch of which rule, containeth the first, and fundamental law of nature; which is, *to seek peace, and follow it.* The second, the sum of the right of nature; which is, *by all means we can, to defend ourselves.* [Hobbes's emphasis][7]

Locke wrote:

> The state of nature has a law of nature to govern it, which obliges every one; and reason, which is that law, teaches all mankind who will but consult it that, being all equal and independent, no one ought to harm another in his life, health, liberty, or possessions; . . .[8]

And, "I easily grant that civil government is the proper remedy for the inconveniences of the state of nature, which must cer-

4. Thomas Aquinas, *Summa Theologica*, Q. 91. Art. 2.
5. Thomas Hobbes, *Leviathan*, 103 (ch. 14).
6. Quoted in Richard Tuck, *Natural Rights Theories*, 120.
7. Hobbes, *Leviathan*, 103–104, (ch. 14).
8. John Locke, *Second Treatise of Government*, 5. (ch. II, sec. 6).

tainly be great where men may be judges in their own case.
. . ."[9] And

> . . . yet it is certain that there is such a law, and that, too, as
> intelligible and plain to a rational creature and a studier of
> that law as the positive laws of commonwealths, nay, possibly
> plainer, as much as reason is easier to be understood than
> the fancies and intricate contrivances of men, following con-
> trary and hidden interests put into words; for so truly are a
> great part of the municipal laws of countries, which are only
> so far right as they are founded on the law of nature, by
> which they are to be regulated and interpreted.[10]

The extent to which theories are alike or different can depend upon the level of description at which we are making our
observations. At a high level of abstraction these theories are
similar in taking reason—our capacity for comprehension, deliberation, and deliberate activity—to be the capacity through
which human beings recognize and endorse fundamental principles of political order. At less abstract levels, quite significant
differences appear. Aquinas's theorizing is part of an overall
perfectionist conception of human beings, and in his view,
complete perfection is nonnatural. In Hobbes's view, the per-
son-relativity of good, the ways it leads to disagreement, conflict disagreement, and a common predicament of insecurity
are grounds for surrendering natural liberty through covenant
to set up a sovereign to preside over the parties to the covenant
and to protect them. In Hobbes's view, the operation of reason
in politics does not aim at the realization of human virtue. That
is a point of sharp contrast with Aristotle and Aquinas, for
example. For Hobbes, reason puts constraints on what would
otherwise be anarchy in which everyone's circumstances would

---

9. Ibid., 9 (ch. II, sec. 13).
10. Ibid., 9. (ch. II, sec. 12).

be precarious. Locke's view is different from both in its emphasis on property as an extension of personhood and the limitations on state power, shaped in large measure by individual rights. In political theorizing other than natural law theory, philosophical anthropology is just as important. Consider Hume and Mill, for example. I have focused on natural law approaches only because they illustrate the main claim so effectively and in many forms.

In tracing the history of natural law theorizing from the middle ages up through the early modern period and more recent times, we can see a shift in direction away from a more perfectionist conception of politics. It is a shift that marks modern political thought in a highly general manner, whether natural law theorizing or not. The prevailing medieval conceptions fitted political life into an overall conception of the metaphysical order in which we participate. In the early modern period, there was a shift to a more rights- and contract-centered conception. There are complex historical reasons for this, and we will not examine them here. But among the changes was the transition from regarding natural law as an inherent principle or disposition of a being possessing practical reason to a conception of what a rational agent would recognize as specifying fundamental liberties and obligations. This is a sense in which natural law theorizing was naturalized in such a way that it was not essentially tied to metaphysics.

Still, it is worth noting that early modern conceptions of natural law, including those developed by Grotius, Hobbes, and Locke, assigned a role to theism but without a great deal of theology. God is the author of the natural law, but it is accessible to rational agents and it applies to all rational agents without mediation through highly specific doctrinal matters. The focus on individual liberty, rights, and property was a quite deliberate project to put political life on a new basis, and one that could be rationally endorsed by those participating in it. Questions of theology, providence, and metaphysics did not cease to be of fundamental importance. However, they no longer informed politics in such a way that the latter was, so to speak, the naturalistic dimension of the former. The notion of liberty became increasingly central. How is liberty to be understood?

III

"Liberty" has meant a number of things. Classical authors lamenting the fall of the Roman republic and the accompanying loss of liberty had something different in mind from what Mill meant or what Rawls meant. In a good deal of the ancient usage, it seems to primarily connote the *polis* or the community or state not being ruled tyrannically, or not at the mercy of another power. It was Athenian liberty in contrast to Macedonian or Persian hegemony; Roman liberty—not the liberty of Romans, but the liberty of Rome—in contrast to paying tribute to another power; and so forth. Liberty was often understood as a condition of a republic, kingdom, or commonwealth rather than a condition or a right of individuals. Moreover, a state could have its liberty while also including different estates and civil statuses, even slavery, for that matter. There may have been many Athenians and Romans who had little individual liberty but cared deeply for Athenian liberty and Roman liberty.

The terms "republic" and "commonwealth" also had wider application than today. A republic could be monarchical in form; the main issue was whether the monarch was one of *us*, rather than one of *them*. A state could have its liberty without being a liberal state. There are ways in which we can speak of the liberty of Sparta, though it was hardly a liberal state.

Berlin remarks of the now most familiar (if still contested) notion of the liberty of the individual that

> . . . the doctrine is comparatively modern. There seems to be scarcely any discussion of individual liberty as a conscious political ideal (as opposed to its actual existence) in the ancient world. Condorcet had already remarked that the notion of individual rights was absent from the legal conceptions of the Romans and Greeks; this seems to hold equally of the Jewish, Chinese and all other ancient civilisations that have since come to light. The domination of this ideal has been the exception rather than the rule, even in the recent history of the West.[11]

Whether or not Berlin presents the history accurately, it certainly does seem to be true that the idiom of individual rights and liberties has been most pronounced in recent history. The conception of liberty as centered on the rights of individuals is a more modern than ancient idea, and it is probably a mistake to look at the history of the concept as a single developmental process in which what was earlier called "liberty" was an attempt to approximate the modern notion.

In addition, there are several different ways in which it has been argued that liberty *matters*. For Hobbes, liberty is a condition for our doing as we wish, thereby pursuing satisfaction of our desires, something we all aim at just insofar as we are appetitive beings. Another is that liberty is a condition for exercise of freedom of the will (on at least some theories) and freedom of the will is essential for attributions of moral praise and blame, reward and punishment. On such a view, it is held that only where there is liberty is there desert and only where there is desert is there justice. Another conception of liberty's importance is that extensive liberty should be permitted in or-

11. Isaiah Berlin, "Two Concepts of Liberty," printed in *Liberty*, ed. Henry Hardy (Oxford: Oxford University Press, 2002), 176.

der to optimize our prospects of finding out and attaining what is objectively good for human beings. We don't have an antecedent or *a priori* account of human good, so we need the broadest scope of opportunity to find out what we can. Another account—similar sounding, but actually quite different—is that *because* skeptical or subjectivist considerations undermine claims to having identified objective goods, extensive liberty should be permitted. This view holds that because there are *not* objective human goods, agents should be permitted to seek good where they wish. Yet another view connects liberty with happiness and virtue because there are distinctive human excellences the achievement and enjoyment of which depend upon the agent's own causality (along with other conditions, as in Aristotle's view). Each of these could be part of a rationale for a liberal political order.

In order for liberty to be a fundamental political consideration, there need not be a single, conclusive answer to the question "what kind of liberty matters most?" It is clear, though, that extensive liberties give scope for people to act on the basis of their own reasons. Liberty enables agents to acknowledge and engage each other most fully as intelligent, rational agents. This makes it possible for individual decisions and public debates to take place *on the basis of good reasons*. Of course, people can have, and can offer, all sorts of very bad reasons for what they do and for what they think others should do. Liberty doesn't ensure noble action, but it protects a sphere of activity in which agents are able to act in accord with what they take to have valuative significance. In the most general sense, liberty matters because it gives us the broadest scope for action on the basis of what matters to us.

We are able to act in a manner responsive to the considerations one takes to be worthwhile or authoritative as reasons for acting (within certain limits). This is neutral concerning the *metaphysics* of value. It takes no stand on whether value is objective or subjective. We know that rational agents deliberate, weigh considerations, plan, decide, and act on the basis of conceptions of what they take to be worth doing or desirable. That is a basis for the value of liberty.

If that is the case, then there are grounds for participants in the political order to have equal and equally protected rights to liberty. I say "right to liberty" rather than simply "liberty" because there are all sorts of conditions that make a difference to the extent to which liberty may be effectively exercised. An agent may have a right to do X in normatively being at liberty to do X, though circumstantially not be at liberty to do X. If I have made bad business decisions that dramatically reduce my ability to borrow money, my liberty is diminished with regard to what the circumstances will permit, though my liberty as a rational agent is not curtailed. There are all sorts of ways my right to liberty can be violated, but untoward circumstances do not, simply as such, constitute violations. There are many kinds of impediments that are not wrongful.

IV

Liberty preserves conditions for the pursuit of many different values and kinds of values. Repressive regimes and illiberal states are alike in shutting off avenues of valuative pursuit and in severely limiting the ways in which people can find worth and significance in their activities. Liberty does not guarantee that there will be minimal friction between different people's commitments, interests, and judgments. To be sure, the extent to which the social world is diverse *and* stable, heterogeneous *and* mutually respectful, tolerant of different ways of life *and* cohesively civil will depend upon many things, including the virtues and vices of its members. Liberty provides wide scope for the exercise of rational self-determination. Rights protecting people against imposition and interference protect their liberty.

In taking their values seriously, individuals, cultural groups, parties, and associations of various kinds often not only want to enact those values, they sometimes also want them to be dominant or exclusive. That is not a defect peculiar to a liberal political order. It is a defect of human beings and a vice that is almost certainly aggravated more rather than less by an illiberal political order. An important task for any civil order is attending with care to making distinctions between offense, disgust, outrage, and harm in ways that respect liberty. Indeed, a liberal political order permits the scope and creates the space for making such distinctions as part of politics, rather than antecedently settling such matters with metaphysics or ideology.

There are those in a liberal order who both benefit from it and condemn it as permissive. It *is* permissive, allowing differences in practices and perspectives and accommodating cultural heterogeneity, but not because it is morally better to have a more diverse society than a less diverse one. It is permissive because of the value of *liberty* and because of the *pluralism* of values, not because of the value of *diversity*. Diversity, just considered as such, does not seem to have any claim on grounds of intrinsic value. If there are multiple and incommensurable sources of value that people can weigh and enjoy in different measures, then liberty is important for making them practically, that is, *effectively*, accessible. There isn't just one way to get judgments of value and worth correct. But I suspect that what is generally meant by diversity is that difference *as such* is to be encouraged and appreciated. If it is difference that *makes* a difference in regard to enriching people's lives and enlarging opportunities for appreciation of value, then it surely is a good thing. But that is indicative of the pluralism of values, not any intrinsic value of diversity.

At the opposite end of the spectrum, those who wish to exclude the pursuit of ends and values that offend or disgust them need to make a stronger case than pointing to the fact that they find those values and pursuits repugnant. They are not being asked to support or welcome them. They are being asked not to regard the presence of those engaged in other pursuits, and enacting other values, as a threat to the integrity of one's own pursuits and values. This does not require altering one's judgment. But it does require acknowledging that one's own judgment has no special claim on constraining the lives of others. There may be reasons of justice for such constraint, but that is not the same issue. Toleration is generally preferable to intolerance, at least when it is not a question of tolerating wrong or perverse values. But attempts to link diversity, value, and liberty in some essential way seem to assign diversity a role it cannot support. That is not to say that it is not related in important ways to essential matters. But the focus on it in many recent discussions of it tends to be an unhelpful distraction from more fundamental matters.

Hobbes is owed credit for an especially important insight concerning the unavoidability of politics and its relation to the issue of the diversity and heterogeneity of people's values. Although it might seem to be going too far to interpret him as a liberal, his conception of the problem to which political thought is an answer is instructive for the defense of liberty. His acknowledgment of differences in people's conceptions of good draws attention to the important fact that it is profoundly implausible to expect people to agree in a comprehensive and stable way on questions of value. This fact is absolutely basic for politics. It points to the result that what is politically crucial is the rule of law and a just civil order. Many differences in judgment about what is worth having, doing, and experiencing will survive any attempt at making such judgments uniform. Human nature will be persistently in the way of that.

Even if Hobbes's subjectivist theory of value is incorrect (and I believe it is) and even if he was mistaken about the state of nature being a state of war of all against all, he had a deep insight into the nature of political life and what necessitates it.[12] Whether or not there are objective values, we cannot expect and cannot count on homogeneity in judgments of value. Political life must come to grips with that fact by a means other than attempting to impose valuative homogeneity. Modern politics, Hobbes theory suggests, should be nonredemptive, governed by the rule of law, and liberal in the sense that it is more rather than less accommodative with regard to people's interests, tastes, and valuations.

This may make it sound as though the case for liberty is mainly driven by Hobbesian pessimism about people coming to stable, widely shared agreements on questions of value. If such agreements cannot be reasonably expected, we should extend liberties as a safety valve protecting security and order against conflict and volatility. There is a measure of truth in this. Liberty can help preserve a political order, whereas efforts to homogenize coercively might further disturb it and render it more fragile. There is, though, a more optimistic, and equally realistic, reading of the same facts. There are many and diverse goods and different degrees of attachment to them. Extensive liberty multiplies opportunities for agents to find, explore, and realize goods, including many that would be inaccessible or practically inconceivable in a less liberal or in an illiberal state.

12. I have argued for an interpretation of ethical considerations as objective in *Choosing Character: Responsibility for Virtue and Vice* (Ithaca: Cornell University Press, 2001) and also in "Metaethics and Teleology," *Review of Metaphysics* (September 2001).

Granted, this can also have unsettling, unwelcome effects. It can threaten tradition, erode customs and customary bonds, lead to fragmentation of world-views, and so forth. But those are not intrinsically bad or necessarily even *very* bad. They accompany change and the multiplication of possibilities for change, and they may create experiential, educational, and aspirational possibilities at the same time that they are discomfiting. Liberty enlarges the range of considerations available to people as possible reasons for doing, wanting, seeking, and so forth. It adds features to the valuative terrain we negotiate in leading our lives. The fact that liberty often brings with it change does not mean that it makes victims of those who do not welcome the change. It may multiply challenges as it multiplies alternatives. But that is not bad in itself.

Politics is unavoidable also in an Aristotelian sense. The view that human beings can only pursue lives of rational activity and enjoy the goods distinctively available to human beings in a political order is fundamentally important. Much of one's education in self-determination depends upon experience and habituation in acting for reasons, weighing considerations, and giving one's reasons. The capacity to do so is not a power that can be simply turned on once conditions are right. It is a realized and effective ability only insofar as it is used and developed. This is a key point that has merit even detached from Aristotle's larger metaphysics. Practical rationality is learned in political life, it does not stand on the side, fully formed and ready to be deployed once there is an opening for it. The potential for self-determination, like the potential to acquire the virtues, is grounded in our nature, but actual self-determination, like actual virtues, must be developed as a second nature through the business of living. It is not simply "there." Lack or loss of liberty not only shuts out opportunities for self-determination, it can also incapacitate people for it. Recent history in the formerly Soviet-dominated countries in Europe is contemporary evidence of this. The habits of mind suited to liberty have to be encouraged and learned, however strongly facts about human nature support the case for liberty. Persistent and systematic repression can keep people from learning liberty and, consequently, keep them from learning politics. It can render people, so to speak, deliberatively and politically incompetent.

This can be overcome, but there is nothing automatic about that and it may be difficult and take a long time. If only power has been acknowledged as politically authoritative (in spite of whatever specious rhetoric has ornamented it), it is understandable that people should see politics mainly in terms of power and coercive force rather than in terms of liberty. To learn the politics of liberty would be to acquire a new second nature, one that cannot be acquired simply by decision.

Aristotle and Hobbes may seem an improbable pair to jointly supply key resources for political thought. But each drew attention to something essential to political thought. Aristotle's emphasis on the naturalness of politics (which is close to what I have more neutrally called its "unavoidability") is as important as Hobbes's emphasis on the fact that people pursue diverse goods because they have diverse conceptions of good.

We should note that there is no especially close connection between liberty and egoism. Indeed, one of the ways in which repressive politics is corrupting is that it reinforces the motive to be narrowly concerned with one's own interests. We often tailor our aspirations to what appears reasonable to expect or hope for, and where liberty is limited, it is understandable that self-interest in the form of selfishness should be increasingly attractive as a mode of deliberation and action. Of course, where there are human beings, there will almost certainly be human beings who are for the most part concerned exclusively with what they perceive to be their own interests. But there is nothing unique to liberty that pushes or pulls people in that direction. There is a central place for *self*-determination in understanding liberty, but that implies nothing about whether what is valued and aimed at is narrowly self-interested.

The form that self-determination takes in regard to concern with the interests and welfare of others (in a liberal order) is a matter for individuals to address in their own terms. Those might involve extensive and multiform concern for others, commitment to shared undertakings, and selfless generosity of time, one's resources, and spirit. Consider various faith communities and voluntary associations to which members are strongly committed in unselfish ways. Also, note that a given individual may be a member of many such associations. It is perfectly possible that in the exercise of self-determination, agents will lead lives in which they are extensively dedicated to the good of others. Self-determining agents can take pleasure in the prosperity and flourishing of others and can have strong bonds of many kinds. The idea that a liberal or libertarian political order requires or results in a social world of only or mostly calculating, thick-skinned, affectively insensible egoists is someone's bad dream. It is neither empirically nor conceptually well founded.

To recapitulate the main claims so far:

1. Philosophical anthropology, a view of the key features of human nature, is presupposed by political theorizing.

2. Two related, essential elements of a plausible philosophical anthropology are that human beings are capable of rational self-determination and that human lives and activities have valuative dimensions—they involve judgments of worth, values to be enacted, critical responses, and the like—*because* we are capable of rational self-determination.

3. Because of the facts indicated in number 2 above, politics is unavoidable for human beings. They must come to grips with practical issues concerning the conditions for leading lives shaped by their values, ideals, judgments, and aspirations. A political order, for better or worse, is an overall set of institutions and arrangements through which the pursuit of values and interests are encouraged, supported, made possible—or not. It is an institutional arrangement reflecting fundamental normative commitments for the society (whatever those commitments might be and regardless of their origin and rationale). We are political beings and not just social beings.

4. Liberty has been interpreted in many different ways, and it has been connected with diverse conceptions of human action, the nature of value, and moral responsibility. There is, though, a main way in which liberty matters that does not depend upon one or another specific resolution of those debates. Liberty matters because it permits and protects the exercise of self-determination through which we enact and engage with what we take to have valuative significance. (This is neutral in regard to the metaphysics of free will and determinism and the metaphysics of the self.)

5. A liberal political order is the type of order most responsive to our capacity for self-determination (which is not necessarily egoist).

6. Aristotle and Hobbes made especially important contributions to political thought. (a) Aristotle recognized that outside politics there are beasts and gods, but human beings need to live their lives in a political order. We are political beings because we act for reasons that we conceptualize *as* reasons, as considerations concerning valuative significance. We learn rational self-determination in leading lives

in interaction with others who also act for reasons. (b) Hobbes drew attention to why politics must accommodate diversity in the conceptions of good that people have. Political order is well served by minimizing imposition of substantive normative order.

7. People are best able to attain and enact considered and informed conceptions of good when they are permitted extensive liberties. Coercive and repressive conditions can incapacitate people for a broad exercise of rational self-determination.

V

Because politics is unavoidable for us, so are questions about justice. Whether we regard it as having specific substantive content or as mainly procedural, human action in a civil condition inevitably motivates questions of justice. And those questions are linked in a fundamental way with the issue of liberty. They are grounded in the same sorts of considerations about human nature and the overall character of human activity.

Creatures capable of rational self-determination (a) can comprehend considerations as reasons for (or against) doing, wanting, having, experiencing X and can do so in a way that involves attributing worth or value (or their opposites) to what is being considered; and (b) can deploy concepts and discursive reasoning in choosing and acting on the basis of those considerations. At the most general level, justice concerns those principles and conditions that distinguish the political order as an order appropriate to the activity of rationally self-determining agents. Political order secures and supports the conditions for liberty, and it does so by being informed by principles of justice. The term "informed" in this usage refers to both basic arrangements and process. Whether or not justice is in fact an actual, felt, living *concern* for someone is a matter of that individual's character. But questions about justice are unavoidable for beings leading lives shaped by valuative considerations.

Theorists who might otherwise disagree on numerous substantive points (consider Mill and Locke, for example) can agree that liberty within the parameters of justice—within an institutionally realized and normatively sound rule of law—constitutes the civil condition. Without justice informing the civil world, the exercise of liberty is precarious. Without the administration of justice, the most fundamental condition for pursuing and realizing worth and value in human activities is impeded or defeated. Facts about what human beings *are* provide grounds for claims about the fundamental value of liberty and justice and their relation.

We all have a basic interest in a political, social order that enables us to lead lives of enacting values and pursuing ends. That is what makes justice crucial to the political order. It need not have an essential and specific, substantive aim beyond securing conditions for rational self-determination. It *can* have such aims if participants in the political order decide upon them. But a feature of this conception of justice is that it is not essentially *aspirational* in respect to any specific, substantive aim that is set for it. Its primary concern for the political order is securing and sustaining conditions for self-determination. This is likely to be a very complex and difficult principle to enact. It can be stated briefly, but its simplicity of content is not also a sign that it can be realized with ease.

Many conceptions of justice are essentially aspirational. They aim at maximizing equality, or maximizing average welfare, or improving the condition of the least well off, or ensuring the least difference in which resources are available to individuals, and so forth. Understandably, in aspirational conceptions of justice, *policy* has a key role. There will be a guiding conception or ideal that justice aims at.

There are strong grounds for individuals to have a concern for justice without that also involving a substantive, shared goal to be realized. That does not leave nothing for justice to "be about." It is concerned fundamentally with the political order as an order in which participants act with a view to their own ends (many of which will be shared) and recognize the grounds for others doing likewise as the central activity of *their* lives. Members of the society should respect the liberty of others without that having to answer to one or another idea of what the political order should *accomplish*. The workings of politics may (and almost certainly will) produce various ends and aims for the society, but those cannot be read off of what justice requires as a basic normative concern.

The view bears some affinity to Oakeshott's view of politics. He wrote:

> Politics, then, is deliberation and utterance concerned with civil desirabilities; that is, with approval or disapproval of the conditions prescribed or prescribable in *respublica*. And this *respublica* is the articulation of a common concern that the pursuit of all purposes and the promotion of all interests, the satisfaction of all wants and the propogation of all beliefs shall be in subscription to conditions formulated in rules in-different to the merits of any interest or to the truth or error of any belief and consequently not itself a substantive interest or doctrine.[13]

And:

> Civil association is a moral condition; it is not concerned with the satisfaction of wants and with substantive outcomes but

13. Michael Oakeshott, "On the Civil Condition," printed in *On Human Conduct* (Oxford: Clarendon Press, 1975), 172.

with the terms upon which the satisfaction of wants may be sought. And politics is concerned with determining the desirable norms of civil conduct and with the approval or disapproval of civil rules which, because they qualify the pursuit of purposes, cannot be inferred from the purposes pursued.[14]

The present approach aims at attaining an understanding of politics and justice on the basis of fundamental considerations of philosophical anthropology rather than starting out with the question, "what is politics (or justice) for?" or "what should be sought from a conception of politics (or justice)?" Political life is the overall setting and character of the lives of human beings, of intelligent agents. In Oakeshott's characterization of it:

> Understood in terms of its postulates 'human conduct' is 'free' (that is, intelligent) agents disclosing and enacting themselves by responding to their understood contingent situations in chosen actions and utterances related to imagined and wished-for satisfactions sought in the responses of other such agents, while subscribing to the conditions and compunctions of a multitude of practices and in particular to those of a language of moral understanding and intercourse.[15]

There are grounds for a rational interest in justice (whether or not people also have an effectively engaged *concern* for it) because everyone has a rational interest in enacting their freedom as intelligent, purposive agents. But again, at its most fundamental level, justice does not essentially concern ends achieved by *policy* or substantive aims. It concerns the conditions required for people to enact their freedom in an order in which all have equal standing as free agents.

Rawls argues that "first principles of justice must issue from

14. Ibid., 174.
15. Ibid., 112.

a conception of the person through a suitable representation of that conception as illustrated by the procedure of construction in justice as fairness."[16] Only thus are we assured of establishing the right "connection between the first principles of justice and the conception of moral persons as free and equal."[17] And it is crucial to Rawls's view that first principles and the overall architecture of the moral (and political) order should not be independent of the conception of the person. He argues that Kantian constructivism ensures that dependence. And he says of his approach that "[t]he leading idea is to establish a suitable connection between a particular conception of the person and first principles of justice, by means of a procedure of construction."[18]

It is not clear why a procedure of construction should be the approach through which principles of justice are to be arrived at. Moreover, among contractarian approaches, there will be differences over what constitute the basic conditions of agreement (e.g., the differences between Rawls's and Scanlon's approaches), and there will be differences in the content of what is agreed. Those differences reflect theorists' rival conceptions of what is most basic in a moral or political order. However, the main strength of a contract approach is its strategy of taking anthropology to be crucial, rather than its method of deriving moral or political conclusions. The normative authority of the conclusions reached by rational agreement depends upon the plausibility and implications of the anthropology of those who might enter into contract. What it makes sense to agree to is what correct judgment would con-

16. John Rawls, "Kantian Constructivism in Moral Theory," printed in *Moral Discourse & Practice*, eds. Stephen Darwall, Allan Gibbard, Peter Railton (New York: Oxford University Press, 1997), 256.
17. Ibid., 253.
18. Ibid., 248.

verge upon. The agreement is not what makes it correct. The very project of seeking agreement presupposes a common world of intelligent and intelligently responsive agency. The key issue is not "given what we take persons to be most fundamentally, what would they agree to in constructing a political order?" Rather, it is "what is it about our nature and our lives that make the human world a political order, and what does that imply or justify in regard to political principles and institutions?"

What we do in the political order, what institutions are constructed, and what practices are made institutionally regular are best left to politics itself. The free agency of human beings can lead to different, but legitimate, political results. This is not to say that "anything goes," but that what is acknowledged as politically sound and what is undertaken on a legitimate basis are achieved in and by a political order rather than by a separate project of constructing one. The hypothetical construction can bring important matters into relief, and it can be a powerful representation of the main elements of an account of justice. But as a hypothetical representation, the architecture of the construction depends upon the anthropology of the builders and their reading of the properties of the materials with which they work.

Here it is important to negotiate distinctions between politics, morality, and the goods of a good life. A liberal political order can be defended on broadly moral grounds without those grounds implying that a liberal political order should be extensively committed to substantive moral aspirations in regard to policy. The basic architecture, institutions, and process of the political order—what we might call its "constitution"—are justified as morally sound if it creates and sustains conditions for self-determination. The moral justification of a political order is not chiefly a matter of what governance brings about or what it achieves under the heading of "policy initiatives." There are hard questions about what are the proper moral limits on the accommodation of self-determination. I do not mean to diminish their importance at all. Still, the main points about liberty and justice can be made without also settling specific questions of moral limits.

I noted above that the fact that something is morally right or morally required, or that there are moral reasons in favor of it, is not *ipso facto* a consideration in favor of state power being deployed to realize or support it. In fact, if something is not just morally required or justified, but morally ideal, even that is still not a basis for state power being used to realize it. Some moral ideals may be such that voluntary agency is essential to their realization. Coercive realization would not be genuine realization. And looking to the state to realize ideals may be not only looking to the wrong kind of agency, but also looking to a kind of agency that can do great harm and commit grave wrongs if assigned that task. Additional argument is needed to draw the state into moral matters beyond those that are necessary to supplying the justification of a political order in the first place. State protections and assurances concerning morally basic liberties and rights are essential. But there should be no presumption that, in general, governance should be an institutional means of coercion for the sake of moral ends.

One reason it may seem that the state should be extensively and substantively involved in matters of justice is that individuals, groups, corporate entities, and so forth cannot be counted upon to act justly. The involvement of the state, via legislation, policy, and enforcement, can correct for the lack of virtue on the part of other agents and institutions. Where virtue is absent or defeated, the state can intervene in the name of justice. There is both an expansive and an austere version of this. The expansive version looks to the state as involved *of course* unless there are strong grounds for blocking involvement. The austere version presumes exclusion of state involvement unless there are sufficient grounds *for* involvement. It regards state involvement as extraordinary rather than its being the regular or standard *modus operandi*. In the austere version, even justice being the master virtue of political institutions does not automatically imply that whatever is just is the responsibility of institutions of governance. It *does* mean that those institutions should be just.

People and communities serious about the cultivation and encouragement of virtue and the realization of moral ends often have (or should have) available to them a broad range of practical approaches and opportunities that do not involve coercive powers of the state. Liberty helps provide conditions for those approaches and opportunities. Looking to the state indicates failure to understand that basic point, or it indicates a sense that the virtues do not seem to be at home in the social and cultural world and now need to be matters of institutional policy in the political order. That is a very bad point to have reached. It leaves one to wonder where the political order is going to look to find what it needs to make virtue a policy that somehow will also be more than policy—that will be inculcated and not just imposed.

VI

Although much of the present account is a development of Aristotelian resources in philosophical anthropology, it deploys them in making quite un-Aristotelian claims. Aristotle argued that moral education should be a basic practical concern of the *polis*; he argued that it is a public matter not to be left to the home and the family. The cultivation and excellences of self-determination and the virtues were, in his view, public matters to be addressed as matters of governance. He was concerned that without such administration, tutelage, and habituation, people were not likely to develop and enjoy distinctively human excellences.

But there are considerations in favor of liberty that point in a direction that is different from the one Aristotle describes as proper to a *polis*, and especially so once some of the distinctions Aristotle took to be natural are seen to be neither natural nor defensible. They provide a strong basis for shrinking some of the more aspirational claims of the state while supporting his emphasis on self-determination. The merit and relevance of Aristotle's political thought is even more evident when some of its features, especially those grounded in the cultural and social categories and stratification of his time and place, are sculpted away. That makes it possible to focus on his core understanding of moral psychology and the naturalness of politics for human beings.

Despite my disagreement with Aristotle on the role of the state as moral educator, one reason marshaled in the case against the state having an explicit role in moral education plainly has an Aristotelian source. It is that so much of moral education and excellence in deliberation, judgment, and choice comes through experience in which the relevant capacities are exercised, tested, and applied in the particular situations one encounters. They are acquired in the business of living and not by formal instruction. Although it is of the first importance to develop an ethically sound second nature, it is unhelpful and inappropriate to expect the state to directly cultivate the virtues in individuals. Effective moral education itself can only succeed through the exercise of self-determination guided informally in domestic life, in social life, and in participation in the overall civil order. It is better that the civil order should leave a wide scope for the self-determination through which virtuous habits can be learned and appreciated.

In denying that the state should have a primary role in moral education I am not claiming that individual liberty has priority over all other values. It does, though, have fundamental normative authority *for the political order*. In protecting and enforcing rights the action of the state will be responsive to significant moral issues reflected in law. The state will not be morally vacuous; nor, however, will it have a comprehensive project of moral governance or education because it will not necessarily have a specific substantive aspiration. The institutional arrangements and the rule of law do not also have to support or promote one rather than another conception of a worthwhile life or set of ends and interests as part of a general project of moral education. The state will, of course, recognize and uphold the claims of certain rights.

In addressing this issue, it might help to distinguish political *order* from political *culture*. By the former, I mean the basic arrangement of institutions of governance (and the corresponding legal system). A political culture reflects the prevailing answers to questions such as the following: Do people regard governance, institutions and their powers, and the legal system as levers of political and economic control to be contested over in election campaigns? Do they see those institutions mainly as safeguarding their individual interests or mainly as having aims and purposes in respect to fashioning certain social outcomes? Do people see the state as having the responsibility of ensuring opportunities and the resources for people to pursue their own ends and interests? Do they see the state as being a last (but perfectly appropriate) resort for basic needs being met? Do they see the state as enforcer of a wide or a narrow range of moral matters? In many Western societies, these questions are often raised in clusters, with few free-standing instances. In addition, the clusters are sometimes unstable and exhibit internal inconsistencies. Often, people hold that the state should work at realizing *my* or *our* ends by guaranteeing certain entitlements, but should not do the same for others who make claims to other entitlements that they perceive to benefit them. Political culture reflects a society's political second nature, and although a liberal order can obtain in diverse political cultures, it is clearly supported by, and in turn supports, some political cultures rather than others.

People's expectations of governance constitute an important aspect of political culture. For instance, someone might think, "I've worked hard all my adult life, so in my most senior years, provision for maintaining me comfortably should be ensured by the state. If circumstances, even just long life, exhaust my resources, the state should be a provider." Or someone might think, "If people do not make prudent provision for themselves for the part of life after their working lives, it is not the responsibility of the state to provide for them. It makes ethical and practical sense for some sort of provision to be made, but it is not the responsibility of the state." Indeed, in the political culture of contemporary America (but not exclusively there), such conflicting perspectives are widespread, and their friction can be quite pronounced. Government is often looked upon as a provider simply because it *can* appropriate the resources to support entitlement claims. Yet that power of appropriation (and not just the cost) is actually what is at issue.

An extensive scope for self-determination can be educative in its own right. The nature of the political order could be instrumental in encouraging certain habits, expectations, norms of action, and so forth even if it does not have moral education as an active, specific project conducted through explicit policy. If the state has an extensive role in people's lives and people are accustomed to it, they may become so habitu-

ated to it that they don't regard self-determination as fundamental to leading their lives. That could lead to a political culture of submissive resignation, expanding claims of
entitlement, or both. (It could also lead to a culture of ambi-
tious cooperation and mutual support, but that would be more
of a pleasant surprise rather than what is to be expected.)

If people grow accustomed to the confinement of self-determination to a private space carved out of a larger sphere of
state regulation and control, it is less likely that they will easily
acquire effective capacities for extensive self-determination.
(Again, consider Eastern Europe: but also consider that in
much of it, prospects are probably brighter than in Russia. The
difference almost certainly depends in part upon differences in
political culture reaching back beyond the period of Soviet
domination.) Realizing capacities for self-determination
through the exercise of liberty is itself a crucial part of moral
education. It is a way in which informal but nonetheless genuine development and transmission of political culture can sustain a liberal political order.

It is possible to imagine a society that is culturally quite
homogeneous and has a high degree of agreement on values,
concerns, and overall way of life. In such a society, self-determination may seem less important, with something like social
consensus as central to the political culture. In that case, there
may be few reservations about a state role in moral education
and moral matters as policy issues. But it would be a mistake
to count on homogeneity as the basis of the political order
unless it is to be a more, rather than a less, closed society. As
more diversity and more pluralism almost inevitably make
their appearance, it will become clearer how the civil and political orders need a basis other than contingencies of ethnic
or cultural homogeneity. Other sorts of resources, including
commitment to the rule of law and to respecting rights as ex-

plicit matters of political order, are needed, *whatever* one's ethnic, social, or cultural second nature.

People acquire the habits and dispositions necessary for having an effective, practical concern for justice through various kinds of involvement in many different contexts. Learning may come through explicit teaching or it may come through internalizing norms and ideals without explicit articulation or—more likely—a combination of both. One may develop a good deal of fluency in ethical idiom (or at least acceptable practical fluency) without also being expert in articulation. The key thing is that the acquisition of ethical virtues is not an independent project. Typically, we do not learn them, then as a second step apply that knowledge in decision and action. The learning is in the acting, though critical reflection and guidance can be crucial. Political culture can count for a great deal, and the more successful the political culture is in educating people in regard to justice, the less the political order will need to impose on their liberty.

Overall, I have argued that a case for extensive liberty in the political order can be made on the strength of the case for self-determination, even if (a) we have not resolved the metaphysical debate over free will and determinism; (b) we have not settled on a highly specific account of the nature of persons; and (c) we acknowledge that liberty matters, or can matter, in several different ways. It is not necessary that people have a correct and articulate philosophical conception of their nature, their agency, and their goods and interests. Commonsense understanding suffices for participation in the civil condition and the political order, and it suffices in regard to the education in self-determination referred to in the preceding paragraph. What people do may be strong evidence for truths in the works of thinkers such as Aristotle, Hobbes, and Locke, but they need not be going about their lives with any explicit or articulate attention to theory. Rigorous, sustained inquiry, both empirical and conceptual, will fill out and refine philosophical anthropology. But a scientifically and philosophically sophisticated account is not essential to the conduct of politics.

The main upshot of the discussion in this section is that the civic world suited to the exercise of self-determination, and thereby supplying the basic conditions for individuals to pursue their aims, requires effective principles and procedures of justice as conditions for civil liberty. Rational self-determination in a civic world is the exercise of the ordered liberty through which normatively significant human activity is undertaken. In a political order in which liberty is highly valued, justice is of fundamental concern without the political order itself being essentially aspirational. The political order has normative authority in respect to sustaining conditions in which people are most free to act on their conceptions of good. And because that maximizing of freedoms creates and protects the richest and broadest pursuit of activities of valuative significance to people, there is a strong rationale to be concerned with justice. This is because considerations of justice arise at the multiple interfaces of people's exercise of liberty. There may need to be an extensive project of securing people's rights and ensuring enforcement so that rights and liberties are *effective* and citizens are able to exercise and enjoy them. In that respect, the political order can be said to be aspirational, and that respect indeed is fundamental. But that is mainly the project of constituting conditions for the self-determination of individuals rather than setting about realizing certain state-aims, certain overall states of affairs as proper projects for state power.

VII

There are some familiar and important objections to the view that state power should be limited mainly to securing individuals' rights and liberties and that state intervention in peoples' lives should be extraordinary and clearly justified. One is that such severe inequalities of wealth and power will develop that large numbers of people would almost certainly become disadvantaged, disenfranchised, and, in effect, second-class citizens. Another is the view that *of course* the state should have a substantial, ongoing role in promoting overall welfare and guaranteeing that needs are met with respect to health, education, employment, and so forth. In this view, the government should be a reliable provider. Failure in that capacity would be a serious wrong to all those disadvantaged. Either the wrongness of using the coercive powers of the state to accomplish those ends is held to be less serious than the wrongness of failing to meet them or using state power in those ways is not wrong at all. It is a mistake to think that individual rights and liberties have greater normative authority than the other matters mentioned. Each of these views about the proper powers of the state also makes its claim on the basis of what justice requires. In each of these views, justice has aims that reach beyond securing individual rights and liberties.

The liberal position does not reflect the judgment that people are not to be helped and supported or that participants in the civil order need pay no ethical attention to each other. Liberalism is not unconcerned with welfare or unconcerned with whether society becomes sharply divided into rich and poor or whether disease, injury, and handicap go unattended for lack of means to pay for treatment. What the libertarian insists on is an argument to show that it is legitimate to use the coercive powers of the state to address such issues, keeping in mind that the use of state power *is* coercive and that it causes a contraction of liberty. Nor is the defender unbothered if it should turn out that a very wealthy minority can effectively control political power because of their influence-buying power. In fact, the libertarian is *particularly* outraged by such influence *because* of what it indicates about the institutionalization of power. Many of the issues being influenced should not *be* in the hands of the state, though that is not to say that they can be safely or appropriately ignored.

There may be all manner of joint and collaborative undertakings that are needed and justified and undertakings that promote common goods without also being automatically the business of the state. For example, if one argues against extensive state support for and administration of higher education, it is not because of unconcern with whether people are educated and skilled and can enjoy the various benefits of a high level of education. The "inference to unconcern" is indicative of just how widespread is the assumption that if something is socially needed or very desirable, the state should provide it. But why should we start (or end) there? We should look first at the overall political and social culture—the "moral metabolism" of the society, as it were. That would not only be a safeguard against state intrusion, it is also where the heavy lifting has to take place for some of the most significant kinds of change to be genuine.

That is to say that in addition to the "burden of proof" consideration concerning the proper activities of the state, there is also a moral-psychological point in keeping matters beyond the power of the state.[19] It preserves a wider field for

19. The "burden of proof" consideration that I mention reflects some of the argumentation in Douglas Rasmussen's "Why Individual Rights?" which is chapter four of *Individual Rights Reconsidered*, ed. Tibor Machan (Stanford, CA: Hoover Institution, 2001). Rasmussen supplies an extensive argument

beneficence, generosity, educational efforts of many kinds, and the cultivation of accountability. I am not arguing that suffering is justified by being an occasion for virtue. This is not political theodicy, but a practical point of moral psychology. It could be argued that with the state less, rather than more, directly involved in many kinds of matters, the scope for liberty is at the same time the scope for abuses and injustice that government is not in a position to prevent or redress. That is a tendentious way of making the point that we should expect some people to be unfair, greedy, dishonest, irresponsible, and so forth. That is, indeed, something we should expect. However, there is no *a priori* reason that extensive liberties should tend to make people especially selfish or unconcerned with the welfare of others. As noted earlier, it is not at all clear that liberty's liability to those vices is greater than that of other types of political order.

Moreover, extensive state involvement runs the risk of obscuring accountability and institutionalizing corruption. Even when the state is called upon to meet people's needs or protect them against certain disadvantages, there is no assurance that it will do so effectively, efficiently, and responsively. Nor is there assurance that no matter how ineffective or costly, the policy will be abandoned because once something becomes an aspiration of state administration, it is difficult to remove it from the state's agenda. And there is no assurance that it will position people to more effectively exercise self-determination

---

for the conclusion that "[i]n any political debate or discussion, the burden of proof is on the person who seeks to move from the ethical to the political/legal order." Also, the general argument that I make cautioning against too quickly making moral matters into political matters owes a good deal to the argumentation Rasmussen and Douglas Den Uyl present in their forthcoming *Norms of Liberty: A Perfectionist Basis for Non-Perfectionist Politics* (University Park: Pennsylvania State University Press, 2005). I have had the benefit of reading the manuscript.

rather than motivating them to form an expectation of entitlements. Liberal political order has no monopoly on failures of that sort.

Nor should it be thought that a liberal political order is *amoral*, because it does not seek to enforce morality, at least not in a comprehensive matter. Let's not forget that the rationale for a liberal political order depends upon a basic valuative consideration, the normative significance of self-determination. But if it is objected that *practically* this amounts to the freedom to be immoral, that is to be conceded only in the sense that there may be contentious moral matters concerning which the political order does not have a built-in mandate to address directly. A liberal political order is not amoral or a license for immorality, though it is an order in which some matters of moral contention will not be resolved by the state. A liberal order acknowledges that morality and law are often, and properly, separate spheres of normative authority. There are fundamental moral issues properly reflected in laws concerning rights and liberties, but as a political order, liberalism leaves many matters *as* moral matters rather than also making them legal, political matters.

Why not take the view that the state has or should have the power to enforce morality? Surely, moral matters have the weight and the significance to merit the direct attention of the state. But again, the state is not simply amoral. The conditions that most fully enable, permit, and support human moral and nonmoral excellences are a central concern of the political order. Which excellences and virtues people develop and exercise is not a proper, direct object of state power. Even if a social world and civil order is such that there is widespread agreement on various moral matters (that, let us say, remain contentious in other societies), that is not sufficient justification for the prevailing view on those matters' being coercive. (One of the great lessons of the wars of religion in the seventeenth century was that even if there is to be a state church, that does not make nonjurors into heretics worthy of burning. Souls need not be a direct concern of the state, even if agents, in certain respects, are.)

The genuineness of moral matters does not *prima facie* require state enforcement. Moreover, with only austere state involvement, the negotiation of moral friction and conflict itself becomes an opportunity for hearing out others on the issues— or simply ignoring them and going one's own way, with the understanding that others may respond similarly to one's own values. Nonpoliticized or depoliticized moral issues are not thereby rendered matters of subjectivity or somehow less important as moral issues. They remain fully genuine with whatever weight the morally relevant considerations accord them. They remain fully *moral* matters. Were those issues to migrate from the moral sphere to the political sphere that would not in itself be indicative of their having more weight than was at first apparent. It may be indicative of one or another group insisting that their values and concerns should prevail. Reflection may reveal that there are not good grounds for legal compulsion even if the matters in question are morally weighty. The insistence that "if it's morally weighty, it should be reflected in the law" is far too general and far too simplistic. And so is the suggestion that "if it is not a matter of law, then it is permissible for agents to adopt any moral position in regard to it." It may be an issue for which there are decisive moral considerations pointing in just one direction. There may be more to be gained by a political culture that expects people to respect liberty even with regard to those with whom they sharply disagree. If that level of respect is not forthcoming, there could be at least grudging toleration even without interested, sustained, dialectical engagement.

CONCLUDING REMARKS

I close with some brief culminating remarks. Human beings are capable of activity that they regard as valuatively significant, and it is reason that enables them to be so. It is reason that enables them to fashion forms of civil life that include political order. Reason is the capacity through which we can recognize that the requirements of justice unite agents in a common moral order, even if our individual aims and interests are quite diverse. In some settings, there is widespread and relatively stable agreement on values and judgments of worth. But even where that is the case, it cannot simply be relied upon as a solution to the political problem, namely, the issue of the form and scope of institutionalized, legitimate authority. In most social/cultural worlds, there will be the friction of different judgments of worth, different conceptions of value, and modes of interaction, cooperation, and competition of various kinds. That highlights the necessity for mutually acknowledged principles of permissible action and interaction in the civil order and in governance—the necessity for recognizably legitimate political order. However, the friction isn't what most fundamentally creates the necessity for those principles. Those are required simply by virtue of our being rational. That is one of the main lessons of the natural law theorists, whether or not the most plausible conception of politics includes putative natural laws.

Liberty and justice are, or can be, mutually reinforcing. A political order that protects liberty in a political culture that values and respects liberty can help make effective concern for justice second nature. This is because of how it encourages people in forming habits of rational self-determination, valuing both the "having and giving reasons" element and the "self as agent" element. And that concern to deal justly with others will help remind people of the need for additional considerations to make a transition from "X is morally required" to "X is properly among the concerns of the state and its exercise of power." The more that moral articulateness and dialectic are at home in the political culture, the less will moral requirements need to be imposed by the political order.

Finally, the most basic elements of a sound political order are the rights and liberties of individuals. The human capacity for rational self-determination both creates the conditions that require politics and fundamentally shapes the main elements of normatively sound political order.

BIBLIOGRAPHY

Aquinas, Thomas. *Introduction to St. Thomas Aquinas.* Edited by Anton C. Pegis. New York: The Modern Library, 1948.

Berlin, Isaiah. "Two Concepts of Liberty." In *Liberty.* Edited by Henry Hardy. Oxford: Oxford University Press, 2002.

Den Uyl, Douglas, and Rasmussen, Douglas. *Norms of Liberty: A Perfectionist Basis for Non-Perfectionist Politics.* University Park: Pennsylvania State University Press, 2005.

Hobbes, Thomas. *Leviathan.* Edited by Michael Oakeshott. New York: Collier Books, 1973.

Jacobs, Jonathan. *Choosing Character: Responsibility for Virtue and Vice.* Ithaca: Cornell University Press, 2001.

Locke, John. *The Second Treatise of Government.* Edited by Thomas Peardon. Indianapolis: Bobbs-Merrill, 1952.

McDowell, John. "Values and Secondary Qualities." In *Essays on Moral Realism.* Edited by G. Sayre-McCord. Ithaca: Cornell University Press, 1989.

Oakeshott, Michael. "On the Civil Condition." In *On Human Conduct.* Oxford: Clarendon Press, 1975.

Rasmussen, Douglas. "Why Individual Rights?" In *Individual Rights Reconsidered.* Edited by Tibor Machan. Stanford, CA: Hoover Institution Press, 2001.

Rawls, John. "Kantian Constructivism in Moral Theory." In *Moral Discourse & Practice*. Edited by Stephen Darwall, Allan Gibbard, and Peter Railton. New York: Oxford University Press, 1997.

Tuck, Richard. *Natural Rights Theories*. Cambridge: Cambridge University Press, 1979.

3

Liberty, Gender, and the Family

Jennifer McKitrick

DISCUSSIONS OF JUSTICE within the classical liberal, libertarian tradition have been universalist. They have aspired to apply to any human community, whatever the makeup of its membership.

Certainly some feminists have taken issue with this, arguing that the classical liberal, libertarian understanding of justice fails to address the concerns of women, indeed, does women an injustice. Among these we find Susan Moller Okin, and it will be my task in this essay to explore whether Okin's criticism is well founded.

Susan Moller Okin's *Justice, Gender, and the Family* is a landmark feminist discussion of distributive justice that raises issues no political philosophy should ignore.[1] However, libertarians have tended to ignore it. That is perhaps not surprising as Okin

1. Susan Moller Okin, *Justice, Gender, and the Family* (New York: Basic Books, 1989).

would have us believe that libertarian feminism is incoherent. Some libertarians seem to agree, leading one to believe that liberty is incompatible with justice for women. Perhaps libertarians and feminists agree on the "facts," but disagree on the values. Whereas the feminist is willing to sacrifice liberty for justice, the libertarian is willing to sacrifice justice for liberty. Although the libertarian might object to this characterization on the grounds that the demands of justice would be met by a libertarian scheme, the feminist can equally object that the "liberty" she is willing to sacrifice means liberty for men and domestic servitude for women. Okin finds libertarianism problematic for two reasons: its philosophical foundations and its unjust consequences for women. (She focuses, as will I, on women in quasi-democratic industrial societies.) I will argue, contra Okin, that neither the philosophical foundations nor the possible implications of libertarianism are as problematic for feminism as she claims.

I. OWNERSHIP

One of the philosophical foundations that Okin attacks is libertarian theories of property. Justification of a right to property and of a Lockean labor theory of property acquisition is part of the classical liberal tradition, taken up by Nozick in *Anarchy, State, and Utopia*.[2] Okin's most explicit attack on libertarianism in *Justice, Gender, and the Family* is a reductio ad absurdum of Nozick's views about property. Okin argues that absurd consequences follow from the Lockean labor-mixing theory of property acquisition and the observation that mothers produce offspring via labor.[3] The reductio ad absurdum may be summarized as follows:

2. Robert Nozick, *Anarchy, State, and Utopia* (New York: Basic Books, 1974).
3. Okin, 79–85.

1. You come to own something by mixing your labor with it.

2. Women mix their labor with genetic materials and nutrients, and thereby produce offspring.

3. Therefore, mothers own their offspring.

Add to that the view that you retain ownership until you voluntarily transfer it, and it turns out that we are our mother's slaves.

How might the libertarian reply? As an initial observation, this problem has little to do with the labor theory of property acquisition, which is a theory about how a person may come to own something that was previously *unowned*. A pregnant woman "mixes her labor" with things that are inside her own body. If we grant, as Okin seems to, some degree of self-ownership, it would be highly atypical for something inside of a woman's body not to be owned by anybody. Arguably, a woman owns her uterus, the food she eats, and the male genetic material that is freely "donated." An effortless transformation of these materials into a child would raise the same issues. So targeting the labor theory of property acquisition is off the mark, despite the linguistic connection to the "labor" of childbirth. What is really at issue is the view that owning the parts or raw materials entails a right to own whatever those parts become. However, that is not an explicit tenet of the Lockean/Nozickian view of ownership (though it is plausible that they would accept it, or something like it).

Also note that Okin is assuming a particular theory of diachronic identity that may be rejected.[4] An adult human being is composed of entirely different physical matter than the fetus his or her mother carried. Even if the mother owned the mat-

---

4. For more on personal identity, see Derek Parfit, *Reasons and Persons* (Oxford: Clarendon Press, 1984); John Perry, *Personal Identity* (Berkeley: University of California Press, 1975), pt. 3.

ter that became the fetus, it is not clear that she ever owned anything numerically identical to any subsequent adult. Or, if you believe a human being has an essential nonphysical part that accounts for diachronic identity, the fact that the mother contributed physical matter would be insufficient to establish ownership. Along these lines, a popular poet advises mothers that "[children] come through you but not from you."[5] However, if you believe that human beings are made of matter and that they sustain the same identity from the womb to adulthood and that you hold unrestricted rights of ownership, including rights to own people and to dispose of owned property at will, then you are vulnerable to this problem Okin raises, and you may in the end justify a matriarchal slave state.

However, libertarians need not be committed to such views, including those about ownership. One could accept a Lockean view of how one comes to own unowned nonsentient property, yet not extend that to owning humans. One could consistently hold that there are certain kinds of beings that cannot legitimately be owned. Rational agents seem a likely candidate. Along these lines, one might hold that if a human being mixed his labor with silicon and electronic elements and built an artificial intelligence that rose to the level of a rational agent, that claims of ownership would become problematic. The same reasoning would justify denying women ownership of their adult offspring.

This still leaves potentially problematic implications for newborn, prerational infants. Adding the above restriction leaves open the possibility that mothers own their newborn infants and may modify, sell, or dispose of them, as any other piece of property, prior to the point at which they become

---

5. Kahlil Gibran, "Children," in *The Prophet* (New York: Alfred A. Knopf, 1973).

rational agents. However, even if mothers did, in some sense, own their very young children (and the cluster of parental rights seems not entirely unlike ownership), issues of ownership do not answer all moral questions. Most people believe that it is possible for humans to own animals *and* that torturing your puppy for fun is wrong. Some libertarians have more complex, nuanced theories of ownership than Okin gives them credit for. Libertarians are not committed to the view that the right to own property entails that people can acquire complete dominion over absolutely anything that can be retained through any possible transformation. Nozick himself points out a number of problems with that absolutist approach, notes the complexities involved, and leaves many questions unanswered.[6] So, Lockean theories of property necessarily have the consequences Okin envisions.

II. CONTRACTARIAN FOUNDATIONS

A second philosophical foundation of libertarianism that Okin attacks is contractarianism. Broadly speaking, a contractarian approach attempts to justify social norms by reference to contracts or mutual agreements. Players on the political scene are perceived as independent adults who make rational political decisions based upon self-interest. Individuals have no commitments or obligations to others but for the ones that they choose to take on.

As Okin points out, if the parties to the contract are all independent adults acting on rational self-interest, the relevant population apparently includes neither mothers nor children. And if it doesn't, then either it is not self-sustaining or it dawns on caregivers like a natural resource. In reality, one or more

6. Nozick, 174–182.

people are required to take each political actor from birth to this relatively self-sufficient state. If we tacitly assume that people exist who bear and raise children, then the success of our theory depends on the fact that traditional women's work gets done. And furthermore, the theory depends on this caregiving work being accomplished in a way that yields independent individuals without commitments or obligations. Okin charges that contractarians take it for granted that before, during, and after these mutually advantageous agreements are made, there are women around being caregivers.

By assuming, without mentioning, that there is someone available whose responsibility it is to raise children, political philosophers leave the necessity of caregiving outside consideration, outside the realm of justice. Ironically, although the whole theory is set up to justify people's obligations by what they overtly, implicitly, or hypothetically agreed to, it is expected that domestic obligations will be filled, without even pondering the question of whether any rational, self-interested individual did or would agree to take on the responsibility of raising children. If the self-sufficient, independent political actor is not a reality, then we need to clarify what role said actor is playing in political theory. Or if these real-world facts about human life are not relevant, then it is not clear that a political philosophy for "mushroom men" is relevant for real-world humans.[7]

A libertarian may respond by offering a modified contractarianism, which begins by asking, "Are all of the traditional assumptions about political actors really necessary?" What if we assume that players come to the table with histories, ties,

---

7. Mushroom men spring from the ground with self-interested rationality; Mark A. Lutz and Kenneth Lux, "Commenting on Gendered Economics: Mushroom Men, Straw Men, and Real Persons," in *Review of Social Economy* 53:1 (Spring 1995), 121–131.

interdependencies, and a debt of gratitude to their parents? What if, instead of taking it for granted that women's work will get done, we acknowledge that child care and other domestic work are among the issues that are on the table for determining mutually advantageous arrangements? It is not clear that these assumptions would doom a contractarian project. The agreements people would make under these conditions would be worth considering.

Okin herself offers a modified Rawlsian contractarianism. According to Rawlsian contractarianism, just political arrangements are those that would be chosen by individuals who were ignorant about their particular assets (social status, wealth, talents, etc.). That way, no one would be able to skew social arrangements to their particular advantage. Okin would include, where Rawls originally does not, that the hypothetical negotiators would be ignorant about their own genders.[8] That way, gendered division of labor would not be accepted unless the negotiators would be truly willing to fill any of the gender roles available. Rawls theorizes that his negotiators would agree to the two principles of justice:

1. "Each person is to have an equal right to the most extensive basic liberty compatible with a similar liberty for others";

2. "Social and economic inequalities are to be arranged so that they are:
   a. to the greatest benefit to the least advantaged;
   b. attached to offices and positions open to all under conditions of fair and equal opportunity."[9]

Okin essentially agrees with these principles of justice, but she

8. Okin, 101–109.

9. John Rawls, *A Theory of Justice* (Cambridge, MA: Harvard University Press, 1971), 60.

takes issue with Rawls regarding their interpretation and implementation. But like Rawls, Okin sees their implications as more liberal than libertarian.

However, Rawls says his principle of liberty trumps the difference principle when there is a conflict, and a thorough-going reading of the principle of liberty might generate some fairly libertarian conclusions. In his post–*Theory of Justice* work, Rawls waters down the principle of liberty, in part to avoid just this sort of result, but it is not clear that he is justified in doing so.[10] Moreover, even if we let the difference principle go untrumped, it is not clear that the result must be contrary to libertarianism or economic efficiency. Rawls himself states, "It should be noted that the difference principle is compatible with the principle of efficiency."[11] If libertarian economic theory is correct—a factual question independent of ethical considerations—then a libertarian society would in fact be more likely than any other system to work out to the advantage of the least well off.

Another possible response to Okin is to offer a noncontractarian foundation for libertarianism, such as a utilitarian, Aristotelian foundation. However, as any reader of Okin is aware, she has objections to virtually every political philosophical tradition, so there is no easy escape from her feminist critique.

III. CONSEQUENTIALIST ARGUMENTS

Okin's greatest challenge to libertarianism is not directed against libertarianism per se yet it entails that libertarianism is unacceptable because of the consequences it would have for

10. John Rawls, *Political Liberalism* (New York: Columbia University Press, 1993).

11. Rawls, *Theory of Justice*, 70.

women and children.[12] According to Okin, our current extent of free association and contract and our current social practices leave women vulnerable to an extent that is incompatible with justice. So, according to Okin, restrictions of liberty are needed to achieve justice. If she is right, then a society based on libertarian principles would surely have unjust consequences. Individual men and women making voluntary rational choices in the situations in which they find themselves results in women being unfairly disadvantaged.

Okin describes a cycle of inequality and vulnerability, which might be better characterized as a downward spiral for the individual woman. I will characterize this cycle in terms of a simple fictional story about a couple, Sue and Bob. They are a young couple of equal education. As often happens, Bob, being male, finds a job making somewhat more money than Sue. Sue's employer does not want to invest too much in Sue because chances are she will start a family and devote less energy to work or even quit. Meanwhile, Bob has a chance to transfer for a promotion. Sue does not get a transfer and would end up on the ground floor of a new company. However, the net household income would increase as a result of the move, so the move makes sense for the couple.

Then Bob and Sue decide to have children. Who should care for the children? If that question is even considered, it becomes clear that diverting Bob's energies from his career would severely diminish the family's resources, so it does not make sense for him to be the primary caregiver. Domestic help and day care would cost almost as much as Sue's salary. So even if they are not consciously thinking that mothers are better parents, given their social context and the fact that they both want children, it makes sense for Sue to take time off of work to devote to motherhood.

12. Okin, 134–169.

As a stay-at-home mother, Sue loses touch with her professional contacts and with developments in her field, whereas Bob gets another promotion. After the children get a little older, Sue tries to get her career back on track. She puts the children in day care several hours a week and works part time as an assistant to the person who holds her old job. Sue has little opportunity for advancement. She tries to increase her hours, but when her child is sick, she has to leave work. She cannot stay late because the day care closes at 5 P.M. She is not getting ahead as she had hoped, and the housework is piling up. Sue asks Bob for help with the children and around the house. He does not refuse, but mentions his professional responsibilities and little changes. Tensions rise in their relationship. Of course, if she does not like the arrangement, she can leave. She contemplates the personal and financial hardships that such an action would involve and decides that pursuing her career is just not worth it. Besides, now Bob is making enough to support the whole family.

Then one day, Bob comes home and announces *he* is leaving Sue (for someone who is more fun and less demanding). Sue goes back to work full time, out of necessity. She and her children move into an apartment, and now she has to pay for full-time day care out of her meager salary and nominal child support. Bob, on the other hand, has a convenient visitation arrangement and more spending money.

The moral of the story is that the reasonable choices Bob and Sue made together amounted to investing in Bob's personal capital, improving his exit options, and increasing his power in the relationship. Meanwhile, Sue invested in her family and has little to show for it. Although everyone's story is different, the pattern is all too common. Women are caught in a cycle of inequality at work and at home. The expectation that women will bear greater domestic responsibilities leads to inequalities in the work place, which leads to women bearing greater domestic responsibilities, which exacerbate inequalities in the work place, and so on.

Okin locates the major obstacles to women's equality in the gendered division of labor in the home and in the related structure of the workplace, which leaves no time to meet substantial domestic responsibilities. Full-time careers were designed for people with wives at home. This makes freedom from child-care responsibilities a practical prerequisite for professional success. Consequently, people in positions of power tend to be people who are not particularly sensitive to the needs of children and caregivers.

I think Okin has identified a legitimate social problem that arises from people making seemingly autonomous choices. Okin asks: "How can we address this injustice? This is a complex question. It is particularly so because we place great value on our freedom to live different kinds of lives, [and] there is no current consensus on many aspects of gender. . . ."[13] She acknowledges that there is something of value at stake. But apparently, it is a value worth sacrificing: "The way we divide the labor and responsibilities in our personal lives seems to be one of those things that people should be free to work out for themselves, *but because of its vast repercussions it belongs clearly within the scope of things that must be governed by principles of justice*" (emphasis added).[14] Furthermore, Okin seems to think that being governed by principles of justice means being governed by the state.

The fact that Okin thinks that justice requires state restrictions on liberty becomes clear when we look at some of her specific policy recommendations for dealing with the cycle of

13. Okin, 171.
14. Ibid.

inequality. According to Okin, employers should be "required to" ("mandated," "must"): provide mothers pregnancy and childbirth leave; provide mothers and fathers parental leave during the post-birth months; allow workers with children ages seven and under to work flexible part-time hours with full benefits; allow parents of children with health problems or disabilities to work flexible hours; provide high-quality onsite day care for children from infancy to school age; and restructure any demands that conflict with parenthood during child-bearing years. The last is particularly important in academic and legal careers, where the most pressing career challenges traditionally occur when a person is between ages twenty-five and thirty-five. If an employer does not make these provisions, direct government subsidies should be given to lower-income parents with children in day care. And schools should be required to provide high-quality after-school programs.[15] Perhaps Okin's most original suggestion is the following: If a couple chooses a traditional division of labor within their marriage, both partners should have equal legal entitlement to all earnings—employers must issue two paychecks equally divided between the employee and his partner.[16]

IV. LIBERTARIAN RESPONSES

Onsite day care and flexible hours would be great for working parents, and officially splitting the paycheck of the wage earning partner might be an excellent arrangement for some couples. However, mandating or requiring these practices would interfere with self-determination of the terms of our own associations, agreements, and contracts. Okin's recommendations would place substantial burdens on taxpayers, businesses,

15. Ibid., 176–177.
16. Ibid., 181.

and employers and would probably have various unwanted consequences. For example, new detection and enforcement mechanisms would be required to oversee marital financial arrangements. So perhaps Okin's recommendations are too interventionist, restrictive, or impractical—the cure is worse than the disease.

But even if that is so, Okin's diagnosis still stands, and at this point, it seems to me that libertarians have basically two ways to respond. One is to grant that under the present gender system, people making free choices about work and family results in a situation in which women are "differently advantaged" and that it would require substantial interference with personal liberty to alter this situation. But, the libertarian argues, such interferences are unacceptable. So, unfortunately for women, that is just the way it is. And unfortunately, many libertarians seem to have this response. They hail the traditional gendered division of labor as marvelously efficient or "natural" or acquiesce to it as inevitable or beyond question, and they seem oblivious or insensitive to the vulnerabilities it creates. A classic example of this is John Stuart Mill, whose *On Liberty* places him within the classical liberal tradition.[17] In *The Subjection of Women*, Mill spends one hundred pages brilliantly arguing that we have no reason to believe that women and men have different natural abilities, nor that gender inequalities are justifiable.[18] Furthermore, he is aware that earning power can translate into dominance. Mill says, "There will naturally also be a more potential voice on the side, whichever it is, that brings the means of support."[19] However, as forward-looking

17. John Stuart Mill, *On Liberty* (New York: Penguin Books, 1975).
18. John Stuart Mill, *The Subjection of Women* (New York: Prometheus Books, 1986).
19. Mill, *Subjection*, 46.

as his views on women were, he could not envision any alternative to the traditional gendered division of labor. Mill says:

> When the support of the family depends . . . on the earnings, the common arrangement, by which the man earns the income and the wife superintends the domestic expenditures, seems to me in general the most suitable division of labor between the two persons.[20]

Shortly after, he says more strongly, "It is not . . . a desirable custom that the wife should contribute by her labor to the income of the family . . ." because the children would not be properly cared for.[21] For Mill, getting married and having children is a career choice for a woman. Mill says:

> Like a man when he chooses a profession, so, when a woman marries, it may in general be understood that she makes a choice of the management of a household, and the bringing up of a family, as the first call upon her exertions, during as many years of her life as may be required for the purpose; and that she renounces . . . all which are not consistent with the requirements of this.[22]

But getting married and having children is not a career choice for a man. The husband has a wage-earning career *and* a family. Mill inexplicably adopts a double standard here, which he so eloquently rejects in every other context.

One might say that despite being ahead of his time in many ways, Mill was a product of his day. But contemporary libertarians seem to have the same mental block. Once, at a Liberty Fund conference, a participant asked, "Why do married women work?" I retorted, "Why do you ask why married *women* work?" He replied, "Because I just assumed that single

---

20. Ibid., 53.
21. Ibid.
22. Ibid., 54.

women would have to work." I was dumbfounded, trying to process this nonsequitur. Then I realized he had assumed the relevant contrast class of married women was single women, and he could not conceive of anyone asking "why do married men work?" even when prompted. The moment passed, and it seemed that no one in the room grasped the import of my question.

If libertarianism is unconcerned about the traditional gendered division of labor and all of the vulnerability for women that it entails, then it *should* be shunned by feminists. Some libertarians might say "good riddance," but the point is that they are apparently content with a system that does not provide equal opportunities for women, which seems to be in tension with the Libertarian Party platform:

> As Libertarians, we seek a world of liberty; a world in which all individuals are sovereign over their own lives, and no one is forced to sacrifice his or her values for the benefit of others.[23]

A patriarchal world is not one in which women are sovereign over their own lives. And although overt physical force is not always used, the gender system promotes and depends on the expectation that women will sacrifice their values for the benefit of others.

So, the first line of response is woefully inadequate, for it is hardly a response at all. It amounts to basically being oblivious or turning a blind eye to the issues Okin raises. If that is the best that libertarians can do, they are proper subjects of feminist criticism. A better libertarian approach would be to acknowledge the Okin has identified some serious difficulties, but that state intervention is neither the only nor the best way

23. National Platform of the Libertarian Party, http://www.lp.org/issues/platform_all.shtml.

to deal with them. In order to do this, however, libertarians have to offer other strategies for dealing with the cycle of inequality. The problem, for rhetorical purposes anyway, is that there is not, nor can there be, a grand libertarian plan for coordinating and changing behavior, of employers and individuals, both in their private and professional lives. Perhaps educational, consciousness-raising programs could be initiated, alerting women to the risks of vulnerability by marriage. However, a great deal of the impetus for change needs to come from the individual and at the grassroots level.

Again, the difficulties Okin brings to our attention are very real, and it does not diminish their significance at all to suggest that different people can have different and creative ways of dealing with them in their own lives. Okin seems to have greater confidence in the ability of government to manage women's lives than in the ability of women to protect their own interests. Perhaps historically women have been unable to effectively protect their interests, but the failure of governments to protect the interests of women is much worse. To offer alternatives, libertarians can brainstorm about possible strategies that individuals may employ, not because women cannot think for themselves, but to show that there are ways to combat the cycle of inequality without restricting liberty. These are practical, even mundane suggestions, but Okin presents what is essentially a practical problem—how can a woman be a parent without becoming economically dependent and vulnerable?

Different particular solutions are suitable for different individual circumstances, opportunities and aspirations. Some people can work out mutually advantageous arrangements with employers, individually or collectively. Some employers find, for reasons other than coercion, that it is in their interest to enable their employees to meet other commitments. In some careers, women can freelance or work at home. Careers in education are particularly suitable for someone who wants to raise children, since the hours can accommodate caring for school-age children. Nursing is another profession with flexible hours, and pays well with good benefits, even for part-time employment.

Another possible strategy is to invest in one's own education while one's children are young. Colleges and universities offer courses at various hours, and it is usually possible to co-ordinate with daycare or elementary school schedules. A parent can go less than full time depending on her other commitments, and she can study and write at home at opportune moments. (I speak from experience: I began my higher education when my son was three, and he attended my public Ph.D. defense when he was fifteen.)

However, we need to stop thinking of balancing work and family as just a women's issue and start thinking of it as a parent's issue. That means getting rid of the assumption that the woman's responsibility is domestic and the man's responsibility is financial. That is not to say that in the best possible world, all parents have careers.

Being free of the necessity to earn income is often a desirable circumstance for anyone, especially for a parent of a young child. But it is important that parents work out an arrangement to minimize vulnerability for the non–wage-earning parent.

V. MARRIAGE CONTRACTS

Okin laments the current state of family law, which puts women and children at a disdvantage.[24] An alternative would be to allow people to work out their own arrangements. For-

24. Okin, 163.

mally dividing the wage-earner's paycheck is one such possible arrangement, but other types of marriage contracts may be mutually advantageous for different people. However, Okin is suspicious of independent marriage contracts. One might object to marriage contracts on the grounds that they make what should be a romantic union into a business transaction. However, that is not Okin's worry. She has no qualms about bringing considerations of justice into the private sphere and worries that appeals to emotion and unconditional giving are tools that consign women to their traditional gender roles. Instead, Okin's worry about the idea that couples can make their own marriage contracts is that they take insufficient account of the history of gender in our culture, our own psychologies, the present inequalities between the sexes, and the well-being of any children involved at any point.[25] The agreement reached by the parents may put subsequent children at risk, children who had no opportunity to give their consent. She notes that justice is not always enhanced by freedom of contract if the individuals involved are in unequal positions to start with.

With regard to the point about children, the fact is that children are always born into circumstances they did not ask for. Some of these circumstances are fortunate, and some are not. There may be various ways extra-parental forces might want to protect children from circumstances beyond their control, but forbidding parents from forming the kind of relationships they want to have hardly seems the most effective strategy or the most pressing concern when it comes to protecting children against the contingencies of life. Ensuring more substantial child support in the event of divorce pales in comparison to ending physical abuse and sexual molestation perpetrated against children.

25. Ibid., 173.

But a more important question is, why does Okin think that women are at a disadvantage with respect to bargaining in a marriage contract? Okin's reasons seem to be that women have less earning power and that women are expected to, and have been conditioned to, accept contracts on unequal terms. However, expectations change and consciousness rises. Although the wage gap does need to be closed, its current existence need not prevent women from making advantageous arrangements. It should also be pointed out that even women in relatively traditional marriages often manage the household money and make major financial decisions. Power dynamics in relationships are not always determined simply by relative earning power.

Okin notes that men are better off financially after a divorce.[26] Although she is wise to draw our attention to the financial power dynamics within families, if money were all that mattered, then men would have no reason to stay married. Yet many of them do. Many men apparently get something out of marriage that is more important than a higher standard of living for themselves. Studies have shown that married people are healthier.[27] Most men and women want to have children and benefit from a parental partnership. Most men want partners and families and are willing to sacrifice other things they value in order to have a stable family life.

So if men have at least as much to gain through marriage as women do, why would women be at a disadvantage with respect to bargaining for terms of a marriage contract? Is it because men will not get married unless it is on their terms? Or because if left on their own, women will continue to enter

26. Ibid., 161.
27. Linda Waite and Maggie Gallagher, *The Case for Marriage: Why Married People Are Happier, Healthier, and Better Off Financially* (New York: Doubleday, 2000).

into disadvantageous arrangements, oblivious to their own bargaining power? Although that is possible, it is not necessarily true. To have an unequal bargaining position, it is not enough that you start off with less. It also must be the case that you value making the bargain more than the other party does. For example, an employer may start off with more resources than a potential employee. However, if the employer wants to hire the applicant more than the applicant wants to work there, the employer has more to lose by not making the bargain. The applicant can hold out for a higher salary than the employer initially offered.

In the case of devising an individual marriage contract, why should women value "making the bargain" of marriage more than men do? Given Okin's picture of what traditional marriage has to offer women and men respectively, she should expect it to be the opposite. Unless women want to get married more than men do, it is not clear why women should settle for arrangements that increase their vulnerability. When most careers were closed to women, they really were in an unequal bargaining position. Marriage was in many cases their only means of support. But given improved opportunities for women, they need not be financially dependent on men. Even with the current inequalities, many women are in a position to refuse a marriage that offers unequal terms once they come to recognize them as such. The key, I think, is recognizing them as such. While the desire for children is an additional incentive to marry, it is much easier for a woman than for a man to become a single parent, and it is not always worse than being a married parent.

VI. CONCLUSION

None of these remarks should not be confused with those of
the libertarian apologist, who says, in effect, "C'mon, girls, it's
not so bad!" There are serious obstacles to gender equality in
modern industrial societies, as Okin points out. And the problem is not merely a matter of equality, but also of avoiding
harm and of vulnerability to harm. Perhaps we should be more
optimistic than Okin that people can work out just outcomes
for themselves. However, we should be less optimistic than
Okin that our legislators can work out just outcomes for us.
Recent political trends do not inspire confidence.

If sexist attitudes are ingrained enough to make nongov-
ernmental solutions unworkable, it is hard to see why they
would not make governmental solutions equally unworkable.
As Okin points out, there is every reason to believe that those
in charge of writing, interpreting, and applying laws will be
products of the prevailing gender system. When we hand the
government the power to set the terms of marriage and employment, we hand it to people who, by and large, have gotten
where they are by not having to worry about "women's work."
So although it is tempting to construe "the woman question"
as a dilemma between liberty and equality, it is doubtful, in
this instance at least, that sacrificing liberty will make us more
equal. Those of us who worry about what has traditionally been
women's work are in the best position to find ways of seeing
that such work gets done without sacrificing other things we
value.

4

Libertarian Justice:
A Natural Rights
Approach

Tibor R. Machan

PRELIMINARIES ON JUSTICE

"What is justice?" asked Socrates, some 2,500 years ago. We're still asking. And arguing.[1] Significantly different conceptions of justice continue to flourish. Libertarianism proposes one, as do socialism, fascism, welfare-statism and other political philosophies.[2] That we disagree about the nature of justice does

I wish to thank Randall R. Dipert, Ruth Sample, and David Kelley for their critical comments on an earlier draft of this essay. I also thank Katherine Z. Machan for her valuable suggestions.

1. There is no reason to be discouraged by this fact, however. Fundamental issues in philosophy and its various branches are reexamined by members of each generation, in part because human beings do not welcome simply having the answers to such questions handed to them by members of past generations, however wise and erudite those members are, indeed, even if their answers were, in fact, quite right about the matter at hand. Unlike in a science, in philosophy this process of revisiting issues is the norm.

2. This is a bit misleading because among libertarian political thinkers the idea of justice isn't understood fully uniformly. Yet that is true among socialists or welfare-statists as well.

not mean there is no right idea of justice, of course—though to complicate things even more, sometimes it seems we can't even agree on whether we disagree.[3]

In this discussion I will not be seeking a fixed, final, perfect ideal of justice, along lines suggested in some of Plato's dialogues. Nor will some consensus suffice. Nor again the conclusion that no determination is possible. Nor will I be focusing on justice as a personal virtue, in the Socratic sense, but as a metanormative principle.[4] Instead, a conception arising from the most reasonable propositions in various branches of human inquiry will help us reach the right idea of justice.

I am convinced that a natural-law method for identifying principles of right and justice is correct. In brief, I hold that despite our basic individuality, all human beings also share a common nature, an identity, and that the knowable facts about our nature justify upholding social principles appropriate to the life and community organization of the kind of beings we are.[5]

3. In recent years, James P. Sterba has counter-intuitively argued that nearly all supposedly different theories of justice have basic elements in common from which only his welfare-statist conception would follow. I dispute the contention that we really all agree about justice to the extent Sterba proposes, but I will address his argument later in this discussion. See James P. Sterba, *Justice: Alternative Perspectives* (Belmont, CA: Wadsworth Publishing Co., 1991), and *Morality and Social Justice* (Lanham, MD: Rowman & Littlefield, 1995).

4. For an elucidation of this concept, see Douglas B. Rasmussen and Douglas J. Den Uyl, *Liberty and Nature* (Chicago: Open Court Publishing Co., Inc., 1990) and *Norms of Liberty* (College Station, PA: Pennsylvania University Press, 2005). For a summary, see Edward Younkins, "Principles of Metanormative Justice," http://solohq.com/Articles/Younkins/Principles_of_Metanormative_Justice.shtml. For an exceptionally insightful discussion of the evolution of the concept of justice, see Hanna F. Pitkin, *Wittgenstein and Justice: On the Significance of Ludwig Wittgenstein for Social and Political Thought*, 2d ed. (Berkeley, CA: University of California Press, 1993).

5. See Tibor R. Machan, "Law, Justice, and Natural Rights," in *Western Ontario Law Review* 14 (1975), 119–130; "Essentialism Sans Inner Natures," *Philosophy of the Social Sciences* 10 (1980), 195–200; "A Reconsideration of Nat-

Even among classical liberals and libertarians, there are sharp disagreements, of course, and not all are persuaded by the same idea of justice. But natural rights theory is one of the prominent libertarian approaches.[6] Its origins lie in ancient law and have been most clearly spelled out in modern philosophy by John Locke.[7]

"To do justice" means to treat something in a way that is appropriate to its nature or as it deserves or ought to be treated. Ayn Rand has plausibly argued that justice is a species of objectivity, of being factual about something, in this case about the ways human beings ought to treat one another because they are human beings.[8] As she put it,

> . . . "objective judgment" is one of the wider categories to which the concept "justice" belongs. What distinguishes "justice" from other instances of objective judgment? When one evaluates the nature or actions of inanimate objects, the criterion of judgment is determined by the particular purpose for which one evaluates them. But how does one determine a criterion for evaluating the character and actions of men,

---

ural Rights Theory," in *American Philosophical Quarterly* 19 (1982), 61–72; "Another Look at Naturalist Ethics and Politics," in *Cogito* 3 (1985), 75–114; "Metaphysics, Epistemology, and Natural Law Theory," in *American Journal of Jurisprudence* 31 (1986), 65–77; and "Towards a Theory of Natural Individual Human Rights," in *New Scholasticism* 61, no. 1 (winter 1987), 33–78. See also Tibor R. Machan, *Individuals and Their Rights* (Chicago: Open Court Publishing Co., Inc., 1989), in which I consider several of the central methodological issues of normative political theory.

6. Some classical liberal thinkers are not sympathetic to a rights-based defense of liberal justice—see, for example, Anthony de Jasay, *Choice, Contract, Consent: A Restatement of Liberalism* (London: Institute for Economic Affairs, 1991), especially Chapter 3, "Rights." De Jasay, however, has focused on non-Lockean rights theorists such as Ronald Dworkin or on Lockeans such as Robert Nozick, who offer no philosophical support for their doctrine of negative individual rights.

7. John Locke, *Second Treatise of Civil Government* (1776).

8. See Ayn Rand, *Introduction to Objectivist Epistemology* (New York: Penguin, 1979).

in view of the fact that men possess the faculty of volition? What science can provide an objective criterion of evaluation in regard to volitional matters? Ethics. Now, do I need a concept to designate the act of judging a man's character and/or actions exclusively on the basis of all the factual evidence available, and of evaluating it by means of an objective moral criterion? Yes. That concept is "justice."[9]

In this essay it is the application of that concept to the organization of a human community, a polity, that will be at issue. The question I will address is "What is the nature of a just political system?"

Only certain kinds of beings can be said to deserve or be owed justice. Although some environmentalists argue to the contrary,[10] one cannot do justice to a tree, a rock, a mountain or the moon. When defenders of animal "rights" lay out their reasons for believing animals have rights, they tell us about the nature of animals. They focus on what kind of beings they are, on what about their nature warrants our ascribing rights to them and respecting those alleged rights.[11] Justice for the animals consists then of treating them in accordance with standards derived from a consideration of their nature. For example, they contend, among other things, that because animals have interests and a certain type of consciousness, they must not be used against their will.[12] Whether or not a case can be made for animal rights, the proponents of animal rights are correct that there would be no other way to establish such a

9. Ayn Rand, *Introduction to Objectivist Epistemology*, 2d ed. (New York: A Meridian Book, 1979), 51.

10. See, for example, Christopher Stone, *Should Trees Have Standing?* 25th ed. (Dobbs Ferry, NY: Oceana Publications, Inc., 1996). (Answer: no.)

11. See Tom Regan, *The Case for Animal Rights* (Berkeley, CA: University of California Press, 1984).

12. See, however, Tibor R. Machan, *Putting Humans First: Why We Are Nature's Favorite* (Lanham, MD: Rowman and Littlefield, 2004).

case but by reference to the nature of animals. Similarly, to find out what is due to human beings, we must first find out what kind of beings *they* are.

LIBERTARIAN JUSTICE

Libertarians take it that justice consists in establishing and maintaining a political system the purpose of which is to respect and protect the right to life, liberty, and property—and what may be derived from these—of the human individual. (The exceptions are pure positivists who have no account of rights.) Normative libertarians would first establish that such rights exist and deserve respect. Then they would proceed, as a matter of political science, to show why such rights ought to be protected and how they could be—some defending an anarchist approach, others a limited government approach.[13]

What view of human nature underlies the libertarian view of a just political system? At the core is a recognition that human beings are essentially creative, inventive, and choosing agents. To be human means to take the initiative by exercising one's thinking mind, as manifested by intentions, deliberations, wants, omissions, and specific actions, for all of which one can be responsible. The mind of a deliberating human being is not a passive, reflexive or reactive but an active faculty. Individual human beings are distinguished by virtue of their capacity to activate their conceptual form of awareness so as to learn how to live and flourish. They think; and on the basis of their thinking, they do. This is not an intellectualist view of rationality;

13. For the libertarian anarchist versus minarchist debate, see John T. Sanders and Jan Narveson, eds., *For and Against the State* (Lanham, MD: Rowman & Littlefield Publishers, Inc., 1996) and Tibor R. Machan, "Anarchism and Minarchism, a Rapprochement," in *Journal des Economists et des Études Humaines* 14, no. 4 (December 2002), 569–588.

rather, reason is understood as permeating human awareness and judgment, including action, even if it isn't deliberative. Among philosophers who share crucial elements of this view we can list Socrates, Aristotle, Augustine, Aquinas, Descartes, Spinoza, Kant, Wittgenstein—and, of course, Ayn Rand, who has generated perhaps the most philosophically potent arguments for libertarian justice (although she repudiated the label of "libertarian" because of her antagonism to the views some libertarians hold).[14]

Thus, we treat human beings appropriately by, first of all, acknowledging that they are such thinking beings. We do them *justice*, especially in the realm of politics or organized community life, if we don't thwart the rational capacity for creativity, inventiveness, and initiative of innocent persons. I speak here at the most general level. Justice in particular cases must take more specific facts into account (including, obviously, whether a person has committed a criminal act).

JUSTICE AS LIBERTY

A conception of justice that requires liberty in the political realm, in contrast to one that requires "fairness," order, harmony, or welfare,[15] rests on the above view. Adult human in-

14. Ayn Rand, *The Letters of Ayn Rand* (New York: A Dutton Book, 1995), 665. In fact, however, Rand's rejection of this term was arbitrary—her essay "The Nature of Government" spells out a libertarian theory of politics.

Rand uses the phrase "volitional consciousness" by which to designate the distinctive form of human mentality. See Ayn Rand, *The Virtue of Selfishness: A New Concept of Egoism* (New York: New American Library, 1964), 22.

15. For how much in law and public policy is prompted by these and related conceptions and misconceptions of justice, see Thomas Sowell, *The Quest for Cosmic Justice* (New York: The Free Press, 1999). But see also Amartya Sen and Martha Craven Nussbaum, eds., *The Quality of Life (Studies in Development Economics)* (London: Oxford University Press, 1993), in which justice as fairness or equality is championed by the contributors and editors. Interestingly, many overlook the fact that John Rawls, in his *A Theory of*

dividuals possess free will and need to guide their own lives to achieve excellence or to flourish. The decisive issue about justice as a guiding principle of a community has to be human nature and its requirement of sovereignty.[16]

Let me first state the most basic tenets of libertarianism. If these are wrong, then so is libertarianism:

1. Adult human beings (and children derivatively and with proper adjustments) are sovereign over their lives, actions, and belongings. They have rights, among others, to life, liberty, and property.

2. Human beings have the responsibility in their communities to respect and act in recognition of this fact when dealing with others.

3. Human beings ought to develop institutions that assure the protection of their sovereignty, delegating the required powers to agents (governments or the equivalent) for this purpose.

4. Such delegation of powers must itself occur without the violation of sovereignty or individual rights.[17]

5. The agencies to which the power of protecting rights is

Justice (Cambridge, MA: Harvard University Press, 1971), while endorsing justice as fairness, also supports certain basic rights as primary over distributive justice. And he allows, also, that what he would call unfairness is acceptable when it results in overall betterment. Some libertarians even invoke Rawls because they claim the free market system, for example, produces exactly that result.

16. For a comparison between the libertarian and welfare-statist, or "democratic liberal," conception of justice, see Tibor R. Machan and Craig Duncan, *Libertarianism, For and Against* (Lanham, MD: Rowman & Littlefield, 2005).

17. For the application of this to constitutional law, see Randy E. Barnett, *Restoring the Lost Constitution, the Presumption of Liberty* (Princeton, NJ: Princeton University Press, 2004).

delegated must exercise this power for the sole purpose of protecting these rights.[18]

6. All concerns, including the protection of individual rights, must be acted on by members of communities without the violation of those rights.

As with all normative theories, libertarianism has several versions, even though the above tenets are not very complicated. Most libertarian political theorists would not have serious objections against the above claims, although their exact terminology and the theoretical route by which they reach such libertarian conclusions may differ.

LIBERTARIANISM AND INDIVIDUAL SOVEREIGNTY

Libertarians uphold the sovereignty of each adult individual. We hold that persons ought to be self-governing and ought not be ruled by others without their consent.

Libertarians may be distinguished from both the Left and the Right of most countries, both of which enlist government for the purpose of regimenting certain aspects of the life of the individual, demanding that government wield powers far beyond what is consistent with the principles of individual rights. Such regimentation clashes with the libertarian concern for individual sovereignty or self-rule. The Left wants routinely to arrange community life so as to benefit the worst off materially at the expense of the best off, taking the interest of the two to be in unavoidable conflict. The Right does the same thing when it comes to spiritual or mental life because it sees those

---

18. For how this applies to a community's military policy, see Tibor R. Machan, "Defending a Free Society," in *Journal of Value Inquiry* 33, no. 4 (December 1999), 451–455.

elements of human community life as having primary importance.

But because body and soul aren't ever sharply divided—human beings are neither ghosts nor unanimated chunks of meat—the administration of justice by both the Left and the Right necessarily entails regulating both the economic realm and the spiritual realm.[19] For example, when advertisers are regulated in what they may say in commercials (at Leftist urging) and when Sunday blue laws prohibit commerce in liquor (at Rightist urging), violence is being done to the individual's ability to live in accordance with his own values *and* to engage in economic activities. The libertarian, in contrast, sees justification for only those laws that aim at protecting everyone's sovereignty—everyone's right to act on his own behalf as long as such action does not entail violating the same right of others.[20]

Some libertarian or capitalist political economists and the-

19. Ayn Rand noted this a long time ago—she suggested, thereby, that metaphysics has a good deal of impact on public policy. (The Right's idealism and the Left's materialism tend to dictate what they want to be controlled.) See Ayn Rand, *Philosophy: Who Needs It* (Indianapolis, IN: Bobbs-Merrill, 1982), 228–29: "Yet it is the conservatives . . . who proclaim the superiority of the soul over the body—and the liberals who are predominantly materialist, who regard man as an aggregate of meat. . . . This is merely a paradox, not a contradiction: *each camp wants to control the realm it regards as metaphysically important; each grants freedom only to the activities it despises.*" (emphasis in original)

20. Much ink has been spilt on how the phenomenon of negative externalities undermines the libertarian adherence to the right to private property; in fact, however, it is only by way of the concept of private property rights that the idea of negative externalities can be conceptualized—for why would such externalities be negative without their violation of someone's property (and related) rights? See Tibor Machan, *The Right to Private Property* (Stanford: Hoover Institution Press, 2002). But see also Liam Murphy and Thomas Nagel, *The Myth of Ownership* (Oxford: Oxford University Press, 2002), in which the authors argue that resources belong to the public or government and individuals come to possess them as a grant, not a right.

orists do not share the view that metaphysics matters much in political theory. I disagree but leave the matter untreated for now, except to note that underlying philosophical assumptions can be detected in virtually any extended argument for a political position.

PROTECTING RIGHTS: THE HIGHEST PUBLIC GOOD

For the libertarian, the just function of the legal system and authorities is, first and foremost, the protection of individual rights. In this respect the libertarian is close to the vision of politics as understood by the American founders. Alternative traditions—whether socialist, fascist, welfare-statist, or theocratic—all seek to impose various strictures on what libertarians construe as private conduct. The advocates of such views often go so far as to claim that there does not even exist a sphere of legitimate privacy in human life. Much ink has been spilled in debating whether the Constitution protects privacy, but the claim that it can do so only if the exact term is used explicitly doesn't hold water. We need only consult the Ninth Amendment, which states, "The enumeration in the Constitution of certain rights shall not be construed to deny or disparage others retained by the people"; and the support for rights to "property" and "private property" in the Fifth Amendment. Those who withdraw into their private property thereby enjoy privacy and are certainly *able* to protect their privacy unless their right to liberty per se is being violated. (Nor is there a "right to draw the curtains of one's living room" stipulated in the Constitution. But this does not mean that the Constitution empowers government to prohibit or regulate curtain-drawing!)

Libertarians endeavor to flesh out the implications of the Declaration of Independence more consistently and completely than do advocates of other political positions. If everyone really does have the right to life, for example, then a legal order ought to be established that protects everyone against any effort by criminals, foreign aggressors, or the legal authorities themselves to coerce people to live in any way other than as they choose.[21] No official paternalistic intervention, even for the sake of improving some aspect of our lives, is tolerable, whether it consists in bans on drug abuse and smoking in private places or regulation of employment. That is what having an *inalienable right* to life, liberty, and the pursuit of happiness comes to, nothing less. A proper legal order is constituted to secure these rights.[22]

CASES IN POINT

Consider the controversial libertarian position that no one has the authority to prevent a sovereign adult citizen from committing suicide or seeking assisted suicide unless it is demonstrably evident that the person is deranged. Or that adults may not be prohibited from using harmful, debilitating drugs, even ones that may prove addictive. Or that risky activities like mountain climbing, racecar driving, and sexual promiscuity

21. Of course, what constitutes our lives is controversial, at least in some circles. Communitarians like Charles Taylor insist that we belong to our communities and thus the lives we have are not actually ours. See Charles Taylor, *Philosophy and the Human Sciences*, 2 (London: Cambridge University Press, 1985), 188. Here Taylor speaks approvingly of "a principle which states our obligation as men to belong to or sustain society, or a society of a certain type, or to obey authority or an authority of a certain type." I address this issue in detail in Tibor R. Machan, *Classical Individualism*, chap. 14 (London: Routledge, 1998).

22. I wish to note here that *pace* Taylor and others, it is not the case with all classical liberal or libertarian political positions that basic rights are normatively fundamental. Even for Locke, whom Taylor accuses of holding this idea, certain natural laws, ethical principles, are prior to any individual rights, ones that arise from these laws once we become concerned with our social relations.

may not be regimented or banned. In all these cases, the libertarian holds that adults have the basic right to pursue the course they want to pursue, provided they are not "dumping" the damaging consequences of such pursuits on other persons by violating the rights of those other persons.

In short, the *right* to life implies the *authority to decide how to conduct one's life.* Rights are principles identified in the field of political theory that spell out "borders" around an individual's sphere of personal authority. We take the time to identify and establish these borders so that the sovereignty of the individual as a moral agent may be identified, acknowledged, and protected in the midst of a complex social life in which others may attempt to encroach upon that sovereignty. For libertarians, politics and law are justified to the extent that they enable us to resist such encroachment. In order for another to properly cross those borders, the sovereign individual "inside" them must provide those "outside" with permission. Perhaps the least controversial example is sexual intercourse; no philosopher, politician, or editorial writer would claim that someone's sexual need gives that person a right to extract sexual favors by force. But the principle applies in less drastic instances as well: No public authority can properly make one person provide services for another, however vital the services may be. If the service consists of supplying the person with resources he or she wants or needs, those resources, too, may be obtained only with the permission of the owner. (Ownership itself can come about through first discovery and/or use, inheritance, voluntary exchange, creation, and production.[23])

23. For a development of this idea, see James Sadowsky, "Private Property and Collective Ownership," in Tibor R. Machan, ed., *The Libertarian Alternative* (Chicago: Nelson Hall, 1974). See also Israel Kirzner, "Producer, Entrepreneur, and the Right to Property," in *Reason Papers* 1 (1974), 1–17. See

Because that which is owned, even in great abundance, can justifiably belong to a person, to hold that others in dire need thereby lay claim to these resources is wrong. It is to imply involuntary servitude or provision due from innocent persons. It is also to imply that those coercively extracting that which belongs to an agent own the agent's life and, therefore, the efforts that create the resources. Rarely there may be justification to expropriate someone else's resources in an emergency; but such an emergency cannot create a *right* to those resources and certainly ought not determine the principles a government seeks to apply in ordinary circumstances and for the sake of all citizens equally.[24]

---

also Machan, *The Right to Private Property*.

By the way, the now philosophically prominent claim—associated with the work of John Rawls—that something not created may not be owned is bogus: One hasn't created one's looks or inheritance but these belong to none other than the person who has it by virtue of being born with it or having been given it freely. The idea that we all own it if someone hasn't obtained it *deservedly* runs afoul of the problem of the incoherence of collective ownership, a situation that results in some people's de facto ownership and others' de facto subjugation. For more on this, see Tibor R. Machan, "The Lockean Proviso,"   http://www.msnusers.com/TiborsPlaceontheWeb/Documents/ PolPhilos/Lockean%20Proviso2%2Edoc.

24. For more on this, see Tibor R. Machan, "Prima Facie v. Natural (Human) Rights," in *Journal of Value Inquiry* 10, no. 1 (1976), 119–131. See also Eric Mack, "Egoism and Rights," in *The Personalist* 54 (1971), 5–33, and "Egoism and Rights Revisited," 58 (1977), 282–88. When Sterba claims it is unreasonable to require those in dire straits to respect the private property rights of those who could bail them out of their trouble, he is implicitly endorsing a form of ethical egoism. Yet if he universalizes this ethical position, as he surely must, those with the capacity to help also ought to strive to advance their own interest and do so as a matter of choice. This may include helping those in dire straits, as I argue in Tibor R. Machan, *Generosity; Virtue in Civil Society* (Washington, D.C.: Cato Institute, 1998). But if such generosity is to have moral significance, it must be voluntary, not coerced, as Sterba proposes via his theory of positive rights (i.e., the alleged rights of the needy to being provided for by those who are able to do this—which would, via taxation, involve coercing the latter to make the provisions).

RIGHTS AND SOVEREIGNTY

One way to appreciate the issue of individual rights is to focus on the right to private property. Rights identify borders within which an individual may take actions free of the interference of others. Those actions need not be equal in their moral quality, yet no one may stop or regulate them against the agent's will.

In the case of universal private property rights, the borders around one's actions are most clearly understandable because they often consist of actions in relation to objects with clear physical limits. If it is your car, you have the authority to use it, provided the rights of no third parties are violated. Norman Malcolm tells the following story about Wittgenstein that makes the point nicely:

> When in very good spirits he would jest in a delightful manner. This took the form of deliberately absurd or extravagant remarks uttered in a tone, and with the mien, of affected seriousness. On one walk he "gave" me each tree that we passed, with the reservation that I was not to cut it down or do anything to it, or prevent the previous owners from doing anything to it: with those reservations they were henceforth *mine.* (emphasis in original)[25]

The moral: Ownership without the authority to decide to what use the owned item will be put is absurd.[26]

25. Norman Malcolm, *Ludwig Wittgenstein, a Memoir* (London: Van Nostrand Rinehold Co., 1970), 31–32.
26. For more about the precise determination of what belongs to whom, see Machan, *The Right to Private Property*. First acquisition is best understood along lines laid out in Kirzner, "Producer, Entrepreneur, and the Right to Property," and Sadowsky, "Private Property and Collective Ownership." Subsequent acquisition is best understood along lines laid out in Robert Nozick, *Anarchy, State, and Utopia* (New York: Basic Books, 1974), namely, through voluntary exchange. It can all be done without guns or mirrors.
In this connection, critics often introduce what has come to be called the

Similarly, if you have a right to your own life, someone who wants to do something to it must gain your permission—as when you authorize a physician to perform a risky operation or a cabby to drive you to the airport. On the other hand, for example, if you don't want to go into the ring with a world champion boxer who wants to fight you, that, too, is properly up to you and no one else. If you want to smoke, drink, take drugs, climb mountains, or go skiing, you need no one's permission, provided no one's rights are violated by such actions. Libertarianism argues that what almost everybody agrees is true in the "obvious" cases is also true in the more controversial cases. If we ought to respect individual sovereignty, we ought to do it consistently, even when people make wrong choices. If one chooses not to embark upon glorious pursuits but instead to be lazy, imprudent, or neglectful toward oneself and one's best interests, this, though often morally reprehensible, is also something one has a right to do. Voluntary asso-

---

"Lockean Proviso," a condition Locke mentions for first acquisition, namely, that "no man but he can have a right to what that is once joined to, at least where there is enough, and as good, left in common for others." Yet Locke himself quickly makes the following observation, which fully concurs with Nozick's: "[H]e who appropriates land to himself by his labour, does not lessen, but increase the common stock of mankind: for the provisions serving to the support of human life, produced by one acre of inclosed and cultivated land, are (to speak much within compass) ten times more than those which are yielded by an acre of land of an equal richness lying waste in common. And therefore he that incloses land, and has a greater plenty of the conveniences of life from ten acres, than he could have from an hundred left to nature, may truly be said to give ninety acres to mankind: for his labour now supplies him with provisions out of ten acres, which were but the product of an hundred lying in common." (John Locke, *Two Treatises of Government* [London: Everyman, 1993], 133.)

There are, of course, difficulties associated with determining ownership in various spheres of interest—water and air mass, to cite the most difficult ones, as well as intellectual property. Here the libertarian relies on the economic and political processes guided by the principle of private property rights and the common law.

ciation is morally and politically essential to free men and women.[27]

A good example of this kind of objection is laid out by Robert Speamann, in support of an idea articulated by Socrates against Thrasymachus, to the effect that government must be the shepherd of the people so that the people act rightly rather than merely to please one another for profit:

> Socrates had used the image of the shepherd to characterize the ruler in a state. Thrasymachus points out that the shepherd delivers the sheep to the butcher and therefore doesn't have the well-being of the sheep in view. Socrates replies that this end is accidental to the shepherd's art. As shepherd, the shepherd provides for the well-being of the sheep. At the bottom of this is the fact that the best sheep for people are the ones that have also best been able to develop as sheep during their lives. The art of the butcher does not define the art of the shepherd. Precisely this changes in the modern world. Here, the market dictates to the breeder how he is to keep the animals, and in no way is the keeping attuned to the animals' well-being. The viewpoints of the animal protector are external to those of the animal keeper and must be asserted "from without."[28]

In answer to this, the libertarian claims that we must accept the risk that goes with being free, including in the marketplace. Yes, some professionals, for example, will not pursue excel-

27. See Tibor R. Machan, "Is There a Right to Be Wrong?" in *International Journal of Applied Philosophy* 2 (1985), 105–109. For a statement of the view that one has no right to be wrong, see Tal Scriven, "Utility, Autonomy, and Drug Regulation," in *The International Journal of Applied Philosophy* 2 (1984), 27–42.

28. Robert Speamann, "The Ontology of 'Right' and 'Left,'" in *The Public Realm*, ed. Reiner Schuermann (Albany, NY: SUNY Press, 1990), 148.

lence but merely cater to whatever consumers demand. Along with the authority to run one's life, including one's profession, goes the risk that one may mismanage these (although what exactly a professional ought to do in the market is not sufficiently accounted for in Speamann's story).

Certainly malpractice is by no means an inevitable consequence of self-government. The shepherd, for example (taking the shepherd to be a producer or vendor rather than some bureaucratic overseer), ought to act in line with his own integrity. This will not occur as a result of regimentation by government; personal integrity is a voluntary and internal development. The consumer, too, ought to act with integrity and influence the "shepherd" accordingly. They all need to *choose* to do what is right, not be made to behave correctly by dint of government regimentation, although what is right will often amount to a highly contextual outcome, depending on what suits the individual involved in relation to his or her many justified responsibilities and commitments. That is how the libertarian system accords with nature, that is, with the moral—i.e., choice making—nature of the individual citizens of a country. If you are being coerced to take an action, you have not chosen it from among moral alternatives. You have, more likely, merely chosen to avoid being fined or jailed.[29]

Again: no guarantee exists that people will use their liberty to do the right thing. But it does not follow that none will do it, nor that making them do it is a valid substitute. And it is unjustifiably cynical to think that those in a free market would

29. True enough, when one is coerced to do the right thing, one might have done it anyway, but having been coerced makes the matter entirely moot. This is true even if some valuable consequences may come from the coerced conduct. A great deal is made of this by Harry Frankfurt, "Alternative Possibilities and Moral Responsibility," in *Free Will*, ed. Derek Pereboom (Indianapolis, IN: Hacket Publishing Co., Inc., 1997), 156–166 (originally published in the *Journal of Philosophy* 66 [December 1969], 828–839)

not freely choose to pursue excellence while attempting to pre-
pare their wares and services for purchase in the market. The
market is viewed as much too demand-driven by critics like
Speamann. In fact, however, more often it is because of the
desire for excellence that the market provides one with what
is desirable. Rather than merely the mutual pursuit of sheer
and meager satisfaction, the mutual pursuit of excellence by
producer and consumer does often infuse markets.

THE NATURE OF SOVEREIGNTY

Sovereignty is that condition under which a person has the
fundamental right to governance such that others must ask
permission before they may intrude on the sphere being governed. Personal or individual sovereignty, which is what is at
issue here, concerns *self*-governance.[30] Accordingly, when it
does make sense for someone to be governed by others—for
example, during legal adjudication or a medical procedure—
the consent of the person to be governed must be obtained
before that governance can commence. The life of those whose
governance is at issue is *their own* life, it does not belong to
others—whether those others be family, society, nation, race,
ethnic group, gender, or humanity as a whole—even if they
govern themselves badly and even if they waste their life altogether.

People may offer wayward individuals advice, write edito-
rials directed at them, send them letters, try to talk with them—
or bid customers away from them with superior service—in

---

30. The concept "sovereign" relates, historically, to supreme rule over
some realm, including those attached to that realm. Only with the emergence
of individualism would it be applied to self-rule or self-governance. See J. D.
P. Bolton, *Glory, Jest, and Riddle: A Study of the Growth of Individualism from
Homer to Christianity* (New York: Barnes & Noble, 1973).

short, they may approach others in every peaceful way imaginable. But they have no authority to usurp the governance of another's life.[31] Arguably, this is what civilized life is all about: a society in which members are expected to treat one another as citizens, not subjects, and in which those who fail to do so are brought to book as criminals for violating the rights of others.

WHAT ABOUT THE POOR AND HELPLESS?

There are other risks of rights protection that have been held intolerable by some critics of libertarianism. James P. Sterba has argued in many forums that the risk posed to the innocent poor or helpless who cannot find help in society based on voluntary contributions is morally intolerable and ought not to be legally tolerated. His argument is that libertarian rights protection asks these individuals to accept what is unreasonable to ask anyone to accept: to respect the private property of the very rich even as they are threatened with devastation.[32]

Sterba says that because of this unacceptable situation—such that it would be unreasonable to insist that those scraping to survive refrain from taking the property of the rich—the innocent poor or helpless have a right to welfare, namely, to

31. Some exceptions include when a person has become crucially incapacitated. Even in the case of punishing criminals, it is arguable from the libertarian position that the criminals have chosen or implicitly consented to be punished given the rational implication of their criminal conduct.

32. Sterba has advanced his views in many forums, including Sterba, *Justice: Alternative Perspectives*, his several papers for scholarly journals such as *The Journal of Social Philosophy*, *Social Theory and Practice*, and *Ethics*, his contribution to the volume he organized, Sterba, *Morality and Social Justice*, and another volume he edited, Sterba, *Social and Political Philosophy* (Belmont, CA: Wadsworth/Thomson Learning, 2003), as well as his single-author volume on political philosophy, *Contemporary Political and Social Philosophy* (Belmont, CA: Wadsworth Publishing Co., Inc., 1995).

portions of the wealth of those who have enough for themselves not to miss it. (Sterba calls this "surplus wealth," but he
drops the crucial context of that concept, namely, Marxian economic analysis.[33])

But there is no justification for depriving another of what
belongs to that other merely because one may need sustenance.
No one, no matter how deserving, has a *right* to my second
kidney, even though I may not need it, or my second eye, even
though I could see passably well without it. If indeed I own
my wealth, there is no justification for another's taking it from
me, even if I have plenty or am not making good use of it (as
indeed many fail to do with their talents or other assets).

Sterba also argues that whether one owns something is to
be established by reference to certain distributive principles,
not by reference to whether the person has obtained it without
doing violence to others. One can only suppose that he would
consider it doing violence to others if one were not to help
others when one has the capacity to do so without excessive
harm to oneself. The best rebuttal is to point out that not helping others is not doing violence to them even metaphorically.
If one were dead, those others would still be in need. One then
cannot be said to have caused the neediness and thus has no
enforceable obligation to repair it.[34] To be sure, under certain

33. For more on why Sterba's case fails, see J. Brooks Colburn, "The
Libertarian Cancan," in *The Journal of Social Philosophy* 31 (Spring 2000), 44–
50. My one quarrel with Colburn is his acceptance of the dichotomy between
morality and prudence.

34. See Lester H. Hunt, "An Argument Against a Legal Duty to Rescue,"
in *Journal of Social Philosophy* 36 (1994) and Eric Mack, "Bad Samaritarianism
and the Causation of Harm," in *Philosophy and Public Affairs* 9 (Spring 1980),
230–259. Sometimes, of course, one ought to help, as generosity and consid-
erateness require one to do, but that is different from being legally obligated
to provide resources. One might ask, "What if one's business beats another
in the marketplace and a worker in that other business loses his or her job—
didn't one then 'cause' this worker's neediness?" No. That's because by "beat-

circumstances it would be unreasonable to demand of a desperately needy innocent person that he respect everyone's property rights. Such emergencies can make it reasonable for that person to steal. One can understand why Jean Valjean made off with that loaf of bread. Yet that act would remain an act of stealing, if forgivable or excusable stealing.

But let's recall that hard cases make bad law. When extraordinary circumstances are met with extraordinary choices—for example, cannibalism in the Donner Party[35] or murder in an overloaded lifeboat—we ought not generalize our evaluation of that behavior to all similar behavior in normal circumstances. Indeed, the legal systems of many societies respond to such cases with the instrument of judicial discretion. (Courts sometimes convict rare cases of cannibalism performed under extreme duress only to later pardon the convict.[36])

In point of fact, though, more often than the proponents of welfare programs care to admit, there are systemic ways for the innocent poor or helpless to obtain support without the violation of any individual's right to private property. There

---

ing another in the marketplace" one has in fact been selected by customers, who are themselves free to shop where they want, to trade with one in preference to the other business that now cannot afford to keep its workers employed. Thus the choice of the customer led to the unemployment—a choice that may not be thwarted by anyone. The unemployment, then, is the result of the exercise of the right of freedom of association: just as none has the right to become an un-chosen spouse of another, so none has the right to become an un-chosen trading partner of another.

35. The Donner Party is the name given to a group of pioneers who became trapped in the Sierra Nevada Mountains during the winter of 1846–47. Some of the survivors were accused of cannibalism.

36. I am told, however, that in some parts of France when a person in dire straits steals so as to obtain food, there is a defense to the effect of necessity that exculpates the accused. I am not familiar with the details and can only assume that this is for extraordinary cases and has not generated a general legal right for have-nots to rob from haves. In any case, it should not.

may not be guarantees, but then neither could welfare from state sources be guaranteed, either in a democracy or in any other system. Michael Otsuka has argued that wealth might be obtained for the innocent poor or helpless through the punishment of rich criminals.[37] He has also maintained that such help could be obtained from resources not owned by anyone.[38] So not only would it be wrong to adjust a just human community to help the innocent poor or helpless by instituting systematic breaches of private property rights, but it would be unnecessary.[39]

If we want to enjoy the best opportunities to survive, for ourselves as well as for those who are least well off, we should hope for a society in which the rights of all are respected so that the creation of the means of survival can flourish without arbitrary obstacles. In a free society that does not systematically rob wealthy people simply because they have wealth to rob, persons in dire straits have a much better chance of either providing for themselves or finding charitable help. A rich society imbued with the values of civilization and respect for others is a generous society; it can afford to be.

One reason that Sterba may be tempted to derive welfare rights from libertarianism is that many libertarians have not proposed an ethical theory from which their libertarianism may be derived. However, natural rights libertarianism, which is the one richest in normative content, does not regard the rights of human beings as normatively primary.

37. Michael Otsuka, "Making the Unjust Provide for the Least Well Off," in the *Journal of Ethics* 2 (1998), 247–259.

38. Michael Otsuka, "Self-Ownership and Equality," in *Philosophy and Public Affairs* 27 (1998), 65–92.

39. The only serious exception would be orphaned or severely neglected children, although with the considerable demand for adoptions and the general compassion most people have for children, it doesn't seem likely that unfortunate children would fail to find sufficient support for their flourishing in a free society. (I thank Randall R. Dipert for raising this issue to me.)

Natural rights libertarianism teaches, with Locke, that one must identify sound ethics by which human beings ought to conduct themselves before one can identify principles of community life. I have argued that the ethics of ethical egoism, in terms of which each person ought to (choose to) strive to live life so as to aspire to the fullest development of one's humanity, is the appropriate basis for the natural right to one's life, liberty, and property. Furthermore, because a moral life is a matter of achievement, something one reaches by a long series of choices, praiseworthy adherence to principles of ethics per se may not be coerced. No one may forcibly make another behave the right way—for example, to be generous, charitable, kind, or helpful. The primary goal of the ethical life is personal happiness, achieved through self-development as a good human being. Thus, to coercively bring about the generous or helpful behavior of the rich or anyone else is morally wrong and ought to be legally wrong.[40]

LIBERTARIANISM VERSUS DEMOCRACY

Democracy in and of itself means rule of the people, or more practically, rule by the majority of those who participate in the political process. Democracy is not, however, morally defensible in this form because the multiplication of decisions into a dominant number does not make the decisions worthwhile.

Nevertheless, there is a moral defense of democracy properly understood that is, with its relevant implications and preconditions spelled out, consistent with a libertarian conception of justice. Here I will simply give a sketch of such a defense.

First of all, a moral defense of an institution would involve

40. For a development of the case for the kind of robust ethical egoism or individualism that supports a political system of natural rights, see Machan, *Classical Individualism*.

showing that it is one that human beings ought to establish in at least some circumstances. What is this institution called democracy? It is a social arrangement that involves protecting everyone's right to have input—for example, a vote—in a decision-making process concerning certain public issues. These are issues that pertain to matters that concern every member of the community and do not involve violating anyone's rights. So, clearly, democracy could not pertain to decisions about who to tax, how to redistribute wealth, whom to conscript for anything, and so on. Democracy can only pertain to public matters that do not involve violating rights.

Suppose, now, that human beings ought to delegate certain of their public responsibilities to expert administrators. This can be established by recalling the value of the division of labor. Thus when experts are selected for matches that need to be refereed, all the players ought to be concerned with how good the refereeing will be. In such a situation, all of those in the match (or some of their delegates) would have a right to participate in the selection process. That process, in turn, could be democratic, involve a lottery, or whatever. But since the match involves a lot of people whom the referees would be serving, all these people in some way would have the responsibility and also the right to participate (in some direct or indirect fashion) in the selection process.

There is something very similar to this in setting up the administration of a legal system. Those who fall within the jurisdiction of such administration would, of course, be the citizens (employers) of the administrators. And one way to decide who should do the administrating is by a democratic process. Because everyone involved would be on a kind of equal footing—each person could be subject to the administration process (by his or her own consent, of course)—each person would have a right to give some input (directly or through a delegate).

To put the matter very succinctly, democracy, within its proper limits, is one expression of the right of every individual in an organized community to exert his or her influence upon those matters that are involved in the administration of that community. This is founded, furthermore, on the doctrine of individual rights, which itself is founded on the ethics of classical egoism or individualism.

Yet democracy must necessarily remain a process directed at selected issues in need of administration lest it become self-destructive. Thus, if a democratic process can address a topic such as whether people may own property, or how much property people may own, or who may vote, or what may be done to the losers of an election, that would be the death of democracy itself. It would, first of all, intimidate voters who would fear the results of being losers in a democratic process. If one lacks the protection of his or her basic rights within a legal system, if those who vote in that system are not constitutionally prohibited from making decisions about the lives and properties of other voters, then the vote itself cannot be honest, frank, or forthright, and will become a process of second guessing, fending off, and deceiving. It is for this reason, among others, that the American founders wanted to restrict democracy's scope, and this is why the current efforts to broaden that scope are in fact anti-democratic.

Democracy, as government itself, must be limited, lest it undermine itself, defeat its own purpose. Those who now wish to expand the role of both are kidding themselves and the rest of us, not only about their concern for justice but also for democracy itself.

Only when one delegates authority to legal administrators to do certain things do such administrators acquire proper authority as opposed to mere power to do those things. If the authority is not given, officials must stay out of one's life. That is what having the inalienable right to liberty means.

The legal authority within a given jurisdiction is a kind of referee whose integrity—whose very nature as the referee—would be sacrificed by intruding on the peaceful choices made by the citizenry. The legal authority is properly concerned only with maintaining peace and ensuring that no one abridges individual rights to life and liberty with impunity. This means that if someone's rights are violated, the culprit at least gets punished for the deed. Neither the legal authorities nor anyone else can always prevent the violation of rights, just as referees in a sports arena cannot always prevent foul play. But the fact that foul play is penalized does provide a disincentive. Once a citizen has "broken the rules"—violated individual rights—adverse consequences ought to follow.

As adults, we all have equal status—not in terms of our beauty, wealth, or background, but in terms of our rights. "All men are created equal" means only that we are equal in one respect: we are all equally in charge of our lives.

The libertarian theory of justice is laid out in capsule in the Declaration of Independence, in which Locke's quasi-libertarian political stance is clearly sketched out. The luminous declaration of our rights in that document could be used by Abraham Lincoln, for example, to criticize the Constitution of the United States, which tolerated slavery.

The Declaration was not meant to be a legal instrument like the Constitution, but rather was set out to articulate an unblemished vision of a free society. It made reference to inalienable rights to life, liberty, and the pursuit of happiness and to the fact that the function of government is to secure these rights. (Incidentally, it is erroneous to claim, as some do, that Jefferson's replacement of the word "property" with the phrase "the pursuit of happiness" in the familiar trio of "life, liberty, and property" is a drastic and anti-libertarian move. The freedom to pursue happiness subsumes all the rights that we require to live our lives, including the right to honestly acquire property, then retain it.[41] Nor is it the case that the case for this right to private property depends on a theory to the effect that individuals deserve their property—certainly one does not deserve one's liver or good looks, yet clearly one has a right to these, so none may deprive one of them without one's permission.)

Government or a legal order aims to maintain such libertarian justice when it secures these individual rights, protects them, and acts in terms of them. Such a government is not established to do anything else—neither manage a post office, build monuments, run Amtrak, conduct AIDS prevention programs, maintain parks and forests and beaches, nor educate children.

The libertarian argues that the rule of law is secured via the establishment, via freely given consent, of a system of constitutionally spelled-out negative rights that function as a sys-

41. See, for example, Luigi Marco Bassani, "Property and Happiness in Thomas Jefferson's Political Thought" (paper presented at the sixth Austrian Scholars Conference, Auburn, AL, March 24–26, 2000) (http://www.mises.org/journals/scholar/Bass6.PDF). Nor is it correct to hold that a right to the pursuit of happiness might introduce positive rights because when combined with the first basic inalienable right, namely, the right to life, and with the theoretical provision that rights must be compossible (capable of being protected in a mutually consistent fashion), there could be no enforcement of such positive alleged rights without violating someone's right to his or her own life and liberty. If I earn my living from, say, my spending part of my life on working, then to claim that another has the right to what I have produced via this work is to claim, implicitly, that another has a right to my life.

tem of consistent standards of justice. In contrast to a system aiming to secure both negative rights (to liberty) and positive rights (to welfare), "rights" that inherently conflict, libertarian justice relies on the principles of individual rights to life, liberty, and property to serve as objective standards for adjudicating conflicting claims of legality. It must be stressed that the active protection of such rights does not render them "positive" in the welfare sense, as some critics would have it. (Nor does it mean that individual rights are mere creations of governments!) The protection presupposes that such rights exist to be protected. The protection is not owed unconditionally but secured via payments and other terms at the founding of the covenant between citizens and those who would serve as the legal authorities. One of the terms is that one respect the rights of others.

We can grasp the distinctiveness of the libertarian polity by recalling that, in contrast, many conservatives and social democrats (or modern liberals) endorse minimum wages, social security systems, licensing of professions, regulations of industry, the war on drugs, closer unity between church and state, and bans on prostitution and other vices. Each of these policies champions an unjustified paternalism and prior restraint (i.e., trying to prevent violation of rights by prohibiting other acts that *do not* violate rights). Such policies also risk abandoning the rule of law in favor of a form of rule that is inevitably arbitrary and nonobjective by requiring administrators and courts to juggle positive rights that are inherently in conflict, noncompossible.

The libertarian view of justice stresses consistency and integrity, and it functions to diminish the role of the will of the legal authorities. This is achieved by laying down and maintaining a system of internally consistent, "negative" individual rights as the standards for legal administration and adjudication. Thus, when some case comes to the highest court, the most basic question is whether the various parties have engaged in the violation of such rights and not which of various basic rights ought to be protected. If the argument that a mugger is entitled to grab a purse because he needs the money carries any weight in a court of law, you know you are not in a court concerned with objectivity, justice, and a consistent rule of law. We may contrast the rule-of-law approach with that of the United Nations Declaration of Human Rights, a declaration of mutually exclusive basic rights. The right to freedom of choice, for example, competes with such measures as the right to health care; thus in specific cases, one or the other must be selected as superior, leaving it to the authorities to select which.

RIGHTS AND RELATIVISM

Are the natural rights that libertarianism upholds just a myth? What if, as has been claimed by philosophical luminaries ranging from Jeremy Bentham and Karl Marx to Richard Rorty, they are an ideological invention and plainly untenable? Bentham thought very little of them because he distrusted the reasoning found in Locke in support for basic individual rights. Marx thought they were thinly disguised ideological tools for maintaining the rule of the bourgeoisie. And Rorty thinks they are culture-bound fictions having no foundations at all.

This view of rights is close to a similar position on political principles in general: relativism. When one hears it said, for instance, that for the people of Cuba socialism may be a sound system, whereas for those in the United States it might not be, one is hearing political relativism. Such relativism contends that it is okay for one party or a dictator to basically run the lives of certain people, depending on their particular historical or economic or technological context.

Some African and Asian government officials at the 1996 Vienna Human Rights conference protested the United Nation's endorsement of the very idea of basic individual rights because, they said, those ideas do not apply to *their* society. And there is widespread agreement with this idea on the part of many people in university philosophy, political science, and history departments, just as Rorty believes that we "cannot say that democratic institutions reflect a moral reality and that tyrannical regimes do not reflect one, that tyrannies get something wrong that democratic societies get right."[42]

Is there an answer to all this? Yes.

Obviously, political relativism fails to regard the nature of human beings as determinative of what rights a human being holds; and, perhaps more deeply, it fails to acknowledge that humans do have a common nature as rational beings that is the same in every particular circumstance. But our examination of human activity across the ages confirms this insight. As

42. Richard Rorty, "The Seer of Prague," in *The New Republic* (July 1, 1991), 35–40.

The foundation of Rorty's metaphysics is the claim that nonmetaphysics or antifoundationalism is the correct position to take on any philosophical issue, including morality and politics. The gist of this position is that what guides sound thinking is not some argument that is sound independently of some perspective or community. Rather, what guides sound thinking is the framework of one's community, whatever that community happens to be and whatever its framework happens to be. And no one can escape his or her community's framework so as to get at the ultimate truth of things. Ergo, no judgment as to which community's framework is better is possible, except as an expression of community preference. It is left as an exercise of the reader to discern whether this relativism is entailed by a given community's framework or is being defended by Rorty himself of his own free will. See Richard Rorty, *Objectivity, Relativism, and Truth* (London: Cambridge University Press, 1991), especially the essays "Solidarity versus Objectivity" and "The Priority of Democracy over Philosophy."

long as the species Homo sapiens has existed, it has existed as a distinctive kind of entity. If those in the fifth century B.C.E. were members of the human species, as were those in the nineteenth, and as are those in the twenty-first and will be those in the twenty-third—then that fact of our mutual humanity has certain enduring ethical and political implications. Some principles of ethics and politics would then be universal, that is, applicable to all human beings, including the principle that each individual is a sovereign over his own life. If we do indeed have a distinctive nature involving the capacity for creative thought and self-government, a suitable community life would require that these basic facts about us be as fully accommodated as possible.[43]

Of course, not all thinkers through all historical periods have stressed the importance of individual sovereignty. But this does not mean that individual sovereignty should not have been respected, only that many thinkers paid little attention to it.

There may be many reasons for that. For example, if certain thinkers belonged to a class of people who benefited from treating others as if those others could properly be exploited by force, it's not too surprising that such thinkers might not be inclined to ruminate on the possibility of universal human rights the wide recognition of which would preclude such exploitation. Pointing out to the world that every individual is equally important is not always in a particular individual's vested interest (though I would argue, contra Marx, that nobody is locked into a viewpoint that upholds his or her vested interests, whether economic or any other kind). Leaders of tribes, countries, nations, states, and other political units would

43. For my development of these elements of libertarianism, see Machan, *Individuals and Their Rights.*

very likely lose their standing if it were to become widely known that they are not entitled to their special positions. Individualism, a vital component of libertarianism, would most likely be suppressed even if it came to light philosophically. Fortunately, such suppression is not inevitable, which is why the concept and values of an individual rights philosophy have managed to emerge and infuse our society.

Thus it is no argument against the universal validity of the position that in many societies individualism is not prominently embraced and anti-individualist positions dominate. And given the fact of human nature and what it implies about the best kind of society for human beings, it is still true that no human being should be made to serve the will of another human being against his or her choice. Slavery, whether it is full-scale, partial, or even minimal, has always been and will always be wrong.

HUMAN NATURE AND HUMAN RIGHTS

For human beings, unlike for the rest of the animal world, there are very few instincts on which we can rely to guide us in our lives. We must *discover* how to live and flourish. That's why we need education—we are not born with sufficiently detailed genetically built-in programs that guide us through life as geese, cats, or even the higher mammals are. We have to learn everything—how to eat, talk, walk, drive, and the many more complex tasks that living a human life entails.

The wilds and the rest of nonhuman world—viruses, mad dogs, earthquakes, floods, and so forth—do not always leave us in peace, undisturbed and unharmed. We do often face terrible hardship caused by them. Yet these are problems that do not require the use of force against other persons. At the same time, however, because other persons can impose themselves on us without our giving permission for them to do so, force may be necessary to fend them off. We have the best chance to make the effort to think through the problems that face us and to solve those problems when we live in freedom, undisturbed by violence from our fellows. Instead of interacting with others coercively, human beings are then able to enjoy the fruits of voluntary cooperative interactions, including competing with others, trading with them, and so forth. It is only such a community of voluntary interaction that is suitable to us all.

LIBERTARIANISM AND COMMUNITY

Some critics of classical liberalism and libertarianism have suggested[44] that community life is alien for libertarians. Not so. People flourish best among other people, provided these do not thwart their freedom. We have the right to and we ought to live in communities, but only if this does not involve coercion, compulsion, or some other violation of the individual's sovereignty.

Conservatives like George Will and modern liberals and communitarians unite against libertarians, however, on grounds that their view of human beings is too narrow. Will joins Michael Sandel in claiming that "much damage is done when we define human beings not as social beings—not in terms of morally serious roles (citizen, marriage partner, parent, etc.)—but only with reference to the watery idea of a single, morally empty capacity of 'choice.' Politics becomes empty; citizenship, too."[45]

44. See, for example, Thomas S. Spragens, "The Limitations of Libertarianism," in *The Responsive Community* (1992). See also Amitai Etzioni, *The Spirit of Community* (New York: Morrow, 1995). But see Aeon Skoble, "Another Caricature of Libertarianism," in *Reason Papers* 17 (1992).

45. George Will, "What Courts Are Teaching," in *Newsweek* (December 7, 1998), 98.

Of course, human beings are "social beings." But this does not mean what Marx meant by it, that is, that "the human essence is the true collectivity of man."[46] Rather, it means that human beings live and flourish best in the company of others. Yet this is something that as human beings they must do by choice when they reach maturity; otherwise it isn't a fully human community in which they live.

The social options available are numerous, some suitable, some not. And we are responsible for making the right choice about the kind of social unions in which we will partake. And when prevented from exercising this choice, as in a totalitarian state, violence is done to us even as those perpetrating the violence claim they are promoting the public interest. As F. A. Hayek noted, the "growth of what we call civilization is due to this principle of a person's responsibility for his own actions and their consequences, and the freedom to pursue his own ends without having to obey the leader of the band to which he belongs."[47]

Human beings are properly held responsible for assuming various social roles in life—in their marriages, families, polities, and so on—but this responsibility is empty if not chosen by them freely. What George Will so cavalierly and callously regards as a "morally empty capacity of 'choice'" is, in fact, the indispensable prerequisite of the moral life.

LIBERTY IN CONTEXT

Just as one must flesh out many details to learn the implications of the fundamental principles of physics for dealing with

46. Karl Marx, "On the Jewish Question," in *Selected Writings*, ed. David McLellan (London: Oxford University Press, 1977), 126.

47. F. A. Hayek, "Socialism and Science," in *The Essence of Hayek*, eds. Chiaki Nishiyama and Kurt R. Leube (Stanford, CA: Hoover Institution Press, 1984), 118.

a particular area of the physical world—so in politics, basic political principles do not tell us everything we need to know to achieve liberty, nourish a free society, and improve our lives. The principles provide a framework within which we can act to solve our problems. If we are to solve problems in society, the only thing strictly forbidden in law is the violation of anyone's rights.[48] It is this that constitutes the central tenet of a libertarian theory of justice and must guide any legal order the goal of which is to establish, maintain, and further justice in the life of a human community. Hayek was right to say that "freedom is the matrix required for the growth of moral values."[49]

48. And because people often resist these implications and even deny them, the drawing of them becomes much more controversial than drawing out the implications of a sound theory of the physical universe. When such respect is made difficult because of lack of sufficient understanding of how it might be done, as with certain environmental problems wherein specification of, for example, private property rights is (as of yet) difficult, this doesn't undermine the fact that the proper default position in all public policy must be to respect individual rights. For more on such nuances, see Tibor R. Machan, *Libertarianism Defended* (Burlington, VT: Ashgate Publishing, 2006).

49. F. A. Hayek, "The Moral Element in Free Enterprise," in *The Morality of Capitalism*, ed. Mark W. Hendrickson (Irvington-on-Hudson, NY: The Foundation for Economic Education, 1992), originally written for *The Freeman*, 1962.

Index